CHARLIE MILLER

The Vanishing Verdict Series: Book 2 of 7

Samira, Ethan & Jonas Crime Thriller Series 2

Copyright © 2025 by Charlie Miller

All rights reserved. No part of this publication may be reproduced, stored or transmitted in any form or by any means, electronic, mechanical, photocopying, recording, scanning, or otherwise without written permission from the publisher. It is illegal to copy this book, post it to a website, or distribute it by any other means without permission.

This novel is entirely a work of fiction. The names, characters and incidents portrayed in it are the work of the author's imagination. Any resemblance to actual persons, living or dead, events or localities is entirely coincidental.

Charlie Miller asserts the moral right to be identified as the author of this work.

Charlie Miller has no responsibility for the persistence or accuracy of URLs for external or third-party Internet Websites referred to in this publication and does not guarantee that any content on such Websites is, or will remain, accurate or appropriate.

Designations used by companies to distinguish their products are often claimed as trademarks. All brand names and product names used in this book and on its cover are trade names, service marks, trademarks and registered trademarks of their respective owners. The publishers and the book are not associated with any product or vendor mentioned in this book. None of the companies referenced within the book have endorsed the book.

First edition

*This book was professionally typeset on Reedsy.
Find out more at reedsy.com*

Contents

Prologue		1
1	The Vanishing Photo	6
2	Tracing the Shadows	12
3	Faded Records	18
4	The Revisionists	24
5	Felicity's Awakening	30
6	The Man Who Never Was	36
7	A Familiar Face	41
8	Agent Pierce's Warning	47
9	Shifting Realities	53
10	The Vanishing Victim	59
11	Echoes of the Past	64
12	The Missing Trial	69
13	Samira's Role	75
14	The Witness Who Wasn't	81
15	Disappearing Clues	86
16	The Fractured Mind	92
17	The New Photo	98
18	Felicity's Dilemma	104
19	A Race Against Time	110
20	The Final Image	116
Epilogue		123

Prologue

Prologue:

The photo sat on Ethan Voss's desk, untouched for hours, but its presence had a weight that threatened to break him. The image was like something pulled from the darkest depths of a nightmare, a moment captured frozen in time that should never have been. The crime scene was gruesome—blood pooling around a body, a jagged wound across the chest—but that wasn't what sent the chill down Ethan's spine. The most unsettling thing about the photo wasn't the violence, it was the fact that the murder had never happened. Not yet, anyway.

Ethan leaned forward, studying the edges of the photo as if willing it to make sense. The faces of the victims were unidentifiable, their features blurred, like someone had taken an eraser to the very fabric of their existence. But what made it worse was the forensic evidence that accompanied it—the traces of DNA, the fibers that had been carefully analyzed—all suggested that the people in the photo, the victims, had once existed. They were real, once upon a time.

The impossibility of it all gnawed at him. This wasn't just some twisted joke or an elaborate hoax. This was something far more disturbing. Someone, or something, had manipulated the very fabric of reality. These were people who had been erased. Their identities, their histories, their entire existence had been wiped clean, as if they had never been born.

Ethan stood up from his desk, the photo still in his hand, the weight of it pressing down on him like a thousand tons. His mind raced, trying to make sense of the mounting chaos. This wasn't just about a crime. It wasn't even just about the murder that had yet to happen. It was about something much bigger, something insidious that was quietly erasing the truth, bending time and memory like a piece of paper that could be crumpled and discarded.

The photo wasn't the only piece of evidence that made Ethan feel like he was losing his grip on reality. The case he had been working on for weeks had already begun to show cracks. He could see it in the records that were altered when he tried to dig deeper, the missing files, the vanishing witnesses. Everything seemed to be slipping through his fingers like sand. And every time he tried to grasp onto something solid, it crumbled in his hands.

There was a soft knock at the door, followed by a creak as it opened. Ethan didn't need to look up to know who it was.

"Still staring at it?" Samira Cross's voice was calm but laced with a tension that mirrored his own. She had been his confidante for weeks now, the only one who seemed to understand what was happening. The only one who believed, as he did, that something far more sinister was at play.

"Yeah," Ethan muttered, setting the photo down on the desk. He pushed it toward her, his fingers brushing against the edge of the image, as though pushing it away could somehow make it less real. "You've seen this before, haven't you? People

Prologue

disappearing, their histories erased."

Samira's gaze shifted between Ethan and the photo, her eyes narrowing as she bent closer to study it. She didn't need to say anything. Her silence spoke volumes. She had seen it before, too. The phenomenon wasn't just an isolated incident. It was happening everywhere.

"This isn't the first time," Samira said quietly, her fingers tracing the edge of the photo as if trying to pull the truth from it. "It's the same thing we've been tracking. The people, the witnesses, the evidence… it's like someone's erasing them. Scrubbing them from history."

Ethan's jaw clenched. "But who? Who's doing this?"

"I've been digging," Samira continued, her voice steady. "There's something bigger here, Ethan. I think there's a group behind this, something that pulls the strings from the shadows. I've come across references to something called 'The Revisionists.'"

Ethan raised an eyebrow. "The Revisionists?"

"Yeah," Samira said, sitting down across from him, her voice lowering as though she feared someone might be listening. "From what I've found, they're a secret society of sorts. They believe that the truth is malleable—that history should be rewritten to suit their version of justice. They've been erasing people, entire events, and histories they find inconvenient. They've been manipulating reality itself."

The word 'manipulating' made Ethan's stomach turn. He leaned back in his chair, rubbing his temples as the weight of her words settled over him. A secret society? A group that controlled reality? It sounded absurd, like something from a dystopian novel. But as he looked at the photo, the faces of the victims—erased—he couldn't deny the terrifying truth. What

Samira had uncovered was real. And the deeper they dug, the more impossible it became to ignore.

"This photo, these people," Ethan said, his voice tight. "They're not just erased from records. They've been erased from existence itself."

Samira nodded. "Exactly. The forensics, the DNA—they all point to the fact that these people once existed. But no one remembers them. They've been wiped from the timeline. Their memories have been altered, erased. And whoever is behind it is using some kind of technology or method to pull it off."

Ethan felt a chill run down his spine. It was one thing to investigate a conspiracy, to dig into a case and uncover corruption or injustice. But this—this was different. The very rules of reality were being bent, and Ethan was stuck in the middle of it.

"We need to track down who's behind this," he said, his voice low with determination. "And we need to do it fast. If they can erase people from history, who's to say they won't do the same to us?"

Samira's eyes flashed with understanding. "We're already in their sights, Ethan. Whoever is behind this is watching us. The more we uncover, the more they'll try to cover it up."

"I'm not backing down," Ethan said firmly, his gaze locked on the photo once more. The victims, erased. The people in the photo—who were they? And why had someone gone through the effort to remove them from existence? Why were they so important that they had to be forgotten?

"We'll find them," Samira said, her voice filled with a quiet determination that mirrored his own. "Together."

Ethan stood up, pacing the room as his mind raced. He had a gut feeling that this was just the beginning. If what Samira

Prologue

was saying was true—and everything pointed to the fact that it was—then they were dealing with a much larger force than they could have ever imagined. The Revisionists were manipulating not just history, but reality itself. The stakes were higher now. The clock was ticking.

He stopped pacing and turned back to the desk, staring at the photo once more. There was one thing he knew for certain: whoever was behind this was powerful. And if he didn't find them first, they would erase him too. He could already feel the ground beneath him shifting. His cases—his life—were slipping out of his control.

But one thing was certain—he wasn't going to let them rewrite his story. He wasn't going to let them erase the truth.

"Let's get to work," Ethan said, his voice unwavering. "We have a lot of ground to cover, and not a lot of time."

One

The Vanishing Photo

Ethan Voss sat at his cluttered desk in the small, dimly lit office, the hum of the fluorescent lights above doing little to soothe the growing unease in his gut. It had been a long day—longer than usual—but the photo on his desk was far more unsettling than anything he'd encountered in his career.

He ran a hand through his graying hair, sighing as his eyes drifted over the image once again. It wasn't the first time he'd seen a crime scene photo, of course. He'd seen hundreds in his years as a cop, then as a private investigator. But this one was different. The photo in front of him was... wrong.

The scene was a disheveled, blood-streaked room. The walls were splattered with crimson, and in the center, there was a body lying on the floor—slumped, lifeless. But what struck him as strange were the faces. Blurred. As if someone had taken a pencil eraser to them, trying to make the people disappear.

The Vanishing Photo

Not pixelated or out of focus. Just... erased.

He'd tried to run the photo through every possible filter, every forensic program he had access to, but nothing about it made sense. It was as though the people in the photo had never existed in the first place.

The room was familiar in its chaotic state—he'd seen enough crime scenes to recognize the typical signs of a violent struggle. But the people, those faces, felt like a twisted version of déjà vu. There was an uncanny sense of familiarity, but he couldn't place it.

His mind flickered back to his earlier conversation with Samira Cross, the journalist he'd reluctantly teamed up with on a few cases. She'd seemed agitated, eyes darting around as if the walls themselves were closing in on her. When she'd handed him the photo earlier that day, she hadn't said a word, just left it there on his desk and walked out.

Now, he could feel his pulse quickening as he stared at the image, the weight of the silence pressing down on him.

"What the hell is this?" he muttered under his breath, tracing his finger across the photo's edges. The blood splatters seemed too fresh, too raw. The crime scene hadn't been staged—this was real. But why was there no record of it? No victim's name. No mention in any police report. It wasn't just that the photo was unusual. It was *impossible*. These people shouldn't exist.

Ethan leaned back in his chair and stared at the ceiling, his mind racing. There had to be a logical explanation, a way to solve the mystery. He'd dealt with enough unexplainable cases in his career—he knew the feeling, the sense of being on the edge of something vast and unknowable. But this? This felt like something else entirely.

The phone rang, jarring him from his thoughts. He grabbed

it on the second ring.

"Voss," he said, trying to shake off the lingering unease.

"Ethan." Samira's voice was breathless, urgent. "Have you looked at the photo closely?"

He couldn't suppress the small, uneasy laugh that slipped out. "Yeah, I've looked at it. I think that's why I'm sitting here, trying not to lose my mind. There's something wrong with it, Samira. The faces—it's like they never existed."

"I've been digging," she said, the hint of a nervous edge in her tone. "I'm not the only one who noticed it. Someone sent it to me too, but there's more. I think it's connected to a bigger case… A case that might lead us to something much darker than we realized."

Ethan furrowed his brow, a cold chill crawling up his spine. "What are you talking about?"

"Something is erasing people. Not just from this photo, but from reality itself. There's no record of them. Like they never existed."

He could hear the hesitation in her voice, the weight of disbelief hanging between them. "You're telling me someone is wiping out people from history? That's insane."

"I don't think so," Samira said softly. "I think someone is rewriting it."

Ethan took a deep breath, trying to center himself. He was used to dealing with strange, even dangerous cases, but this felt different. This wasn't just a murder investigation. This was something far more complicated—and dangerous.

"I need to see you," he said finally. "Now."

Samira agreed quickly, and within the hour, she was sitting across from him in his office, looking just as unsettled as he felt. She handed him a folder, the same one she'd left him with earlier, and this time, Ethan saw something new—notes scribbled hastily on the margins.

"What are these?" he asked, flipping through the pages.

"Research," Samira said. "I've been following a trail. It's connected to a group—a shadowy organization. I think they call themselves the Revisionists. They're involved in wiping out certain people, erasing them from history."

Ethan's skepticism was evident as he folded his arms. "Sounds like something out of a bad conspiracy thriller."

"I thought the same thing," Samira replied. "But there's more to this. People—witnesses, potential suspects—are disappearing. I've found reports of them being involved in cases, but there's no record of them anywhere. I'm talking complete vanishment. Like they never existed."

Ethan stared at her, his face a mask of disbelief. But the photo on his desk, the blurred faces, seemed to mock him. Samira was convinced—she was *sure* there was something to this theory.

"Tell me everything you know," he said, leaning forward, his instincts kicking in.

She hesitated for a moment before speaking. "The Revisionists are people with power. People who can manipulate history, selectively erasing events, people, and facts they don't want remembered. They work in the shadows—no one knows who they really are. But I've found connections—lawyers, government agents, even corporate figures involved. They control reality itself."

Ethan rubbed his temples, trying to make sense of it all. "And we're supposed to go after them? You've got to be kidding me."

"We don't have a choice, Ethan," she said urgently. "Look at the photo. The faces in it are the key. They're all linked to someone who disappeared or was erased from history. We need to figure out who they were, why they're gone, and what the Revisionists are trying to cover up."

He nodded slowly. The pieces were starting to fall into place, though he wasn't entirely sure he liked the picture they were forming. There was something deeper at play here—something far darker than a simple conspiracy. The way reality itself seemed to warp around them... He couldn't ignore it.

As they discussed the next steps, Ethan's phone buzzed on the desk. He glanced at the screen, expecting another call from Samira's contacts or perhaps a lead on the case. But instead, the message read: *"This is your warning. You're next. Stay away from the photo. It's already too late."*

His blood ran cold.

"Samira," Ethan said, his voice low and controlled. "We're being watched."

"What do you mean?" she asked, her expression shifting to one of alarm.

He held up his phone and showed her the message.

"I think we've just stepped into something far bigger than we can handle. And whoever's behind this—they don't want us anywhere near the truth."

The room grew colder. Something shifted in the air, and Ethan felt it—a presence, a weight that wasn't there before. It was as if the very fabric of their reality was being unraveled, one thread at a time.

Ethan stood, pacing in agitation. "We need to act fast. If these people can erase people, they can erase us too."

Samira's eyes narrowed. "Then we find them first. We need to know who's behind this and why they're doing it. And, Ethan... We need to find the people in that photo. Before they disappear too."

The Vanishing Photo

The photo—those faces—haunted him. Whoever was behind this was playing a game with the very laws of time and reality itself. And Ethan Voss, whether he liked it or not, was now a pawn in that game.

As the two of them left the office and stepped into the cold night air, Ethan felt the weight of what was ahead. The line between what was real and what wasn't had blurred, and he had no idea how far this rabbit hole would go. But there was one thing he knew for certain: whatever he did next, there was no turning back.

They were already being erased.

Two

Tracing the Shadows

Ethan Voss was used to the weight of silence, but the quiet of Westfall felt different. It wasn't the usual stillness of a sleepy town, where the hum of daily life had simply slowed to a halt. This silence had an edge to it, a suffocating quality that seemed to press in on him the moment he entered.

The town was small, nestled in a remote corner of the state, far enough from any major city to keep its secrets buried. Ethan had arrived just as the sun began to set, casting long shadows across the narrow streets and abandoned storefronts. The first thing he noticed was the lack of people. The streets should have been bustling for a Friday evening—at least, that's what his instincts told him. But here, not a soul seemed to be out. The only sounds were the distant calls of birds and the faint hum of a nearby power line.

Ethan's car rolled to a stop in front of the only open building in sight—a dilapidated diner with a flickering neon sign that read, "The Last Stop." He hesitated for a moment, his fingers brushing the crime scene photo still tucked in his jacket pocket. He had already called ahead to the local authorities, but their response had been... odd. It was as if they didn't want him here, as though they had no interest in investigating what had happened. Ethan's gut told him that the case he was chasing had little to do with a simple murder.

He stepped out of the car, his boots hitting the cracked pavement with a solid thud. The cold air bit at his skin, sending a shiver down his spine. He adjusted his coat and walked toward the diner's door, the low creak of the hinges sounding too loud in the silence. Inside, the dim light cast long shadows across a few empty booths, and a waitress behind the counter barely looked up from her phone when he entered.

"I'll take a coffee," he said, keeping his tone neutral, though he couldn't shake the feeling that every pair of eyes in the room was on him.

The waitress didn't answer right away. Her gaze flickered over him, and for a brief moment, he thought she might say something. But instead, she nodded and turned toward the coffee pot, as if she had been instructed not to ask questions. As he sat down at the counter, Ethan studied her closely. Her expression was blank, her movements mechanical. It reminded him of a woman stuck in a loop—someone who had long since given up on engaging with the world around her.

Ethan let his gaze wander across the diner, taking note of the faded photographs on the walls—snapshots of a past that seemed out of place in the present. The town had its secrets, that much was clear. But the photo, the one that had brought him here, was the thread he hoped would unravel everything.

He pulled it from his jacket and placed it on the counter, careful not to draw attention. It was still unsettling—the blurred faces, the eerie feeling that something wasn't quite right. As his eyes studied it once more, a sinking feeling took root in his stomach. The room in the photo—there was something about it. The angles were all wrong, the lighting too dark. The body lying on the floor seemed too staged, too perfect. Was this a real crime scene, or was someone fabricating evidence?

"You won't find anything here, you know."

The voice came from a man sitting in the booth behind him. Ethan hadn't noticed him before, but now he could feel the stranger's eyes boring into the back of his skull. Slowly, he turned his head, meeting the man's gaze.

He was tall, with a rough-looking face, a few days' worth of stubble on his chin, and a jacket that looked too worn to be practical. But there was something in his eyes—an unsettling calm that made Ethan's instincts twitch.

"Excuse me?" Ethan asked, keeping his tone casual but guarded.

The man shrugged nonchalantly. "This town? It's not what you think. You won't find what you're looking for. They don't want anyone digging around here. You're not the first one to show up, asking questions."

Ethan studied him carefully. The man was familiar with the way outsiders were treated in Westfall. That much was certain. "What do you mean by 'they'?"

The man's lips curled into a slight smile, but it didn't reach his eyes. "The people who make sure things stay quiet. The ones who rewrite the past when it's inconvenient. They'll make sure you don't stick around too long. Trust me."

Ethan's brow furrowed. The man was talking about the

Revisionists, he was sure of it. But how could he know about them? This town was too small for outsiders to know what was really happening. Maybe he was just another local who had fallen prey to the paranoia that seemed to run through this place.

"Who's 'they'?" Ethan pressed, not letting the man off the hook so easily.

But the stranger only leaned back in his seat, his eyes narrowing as though he'd said all he was going to. "You'll find out soon enough. They're always watching."

Ethan felt the hairs on the back of his neck stand up. He had to get more out of this man. But before he could respond, the door to the diner opened, and a cold gust of wind swept in. Ethan's attention snapped toward the entrance.

A woman stood in the doorway, her silhouette stark against the twilight outside. She was tall, with dark hair pulled back into a tight ponytail, wearing a long trench coat that seemed a little too polished for a town like this. There was something about her that immediately set him on edge. She scanned the diner quickly, her eyes settling on him.

Ethan couldn't help but notice how calm she looked. As if she were used to being in control.

She approached the counter with deliberate steps, her gaze locked on him the entire time. The waitress, still lost in her phone, didn't even flinch as the woman took a seat next to Ethan.

The stranger didn't introduce herself immediately. Instead, she simply spoke, her voice low and smooth, but with a tension beneath it that piqued his interest.

"You're looking for answers about the photo, aren't you?" she said. "You won't find them here. Not in this town. There's nothing to find. The past is being rewritten, and you're not the first person to come here asking questions."

Ethan's heart skipped a beat. This woman knew exactly why he was here.

"What's your name?" Ethan asked, leaning in slightly, his suspicion growing with each word.

"Felicity Harris," she replied. Her eyes flickered for a moment, as if she were testing his reaction. "I'm a lawyer. And I think you're looking for something… that doesn't want to be found."

The sudden mention of a lawyer, especially one who seemed to know so much about the Revisionists, caught Ethan off guard. How could she be so sure of the conspiracy, so certain of the town's involvement? And what was her stake in this?

"Why do you think I'm here?" Ethan asked, now more cautious. "How do you know about the Revisionists?"

Felicity smiled faintly, her eyes scanning the room as though ensuring no one else was listening. "Because I've been tracking them for longer than you realize. And like you, I'm starting to realize the lines between past and present are more blurred than we thought. I've seen their work firsthand. I've seen the way they make people disappear."

Ethan leaned back in his seat. The puzzle pieces were starting to fall into place, but something still didn't feel right. Why was this woman so involved in all this? What did she know about the people who were erasing memories and rewriting reality?

"You think they're connected to the photo?" Ethan asked, suddenly piecing together the unsettling connection between the woman's words and his investigation.

"I don't think. I know." Felicity's voice dropped to a whisper. "And if you keep looking, if you keep asking, they'll make sure you disappear too."

The warning was clear, but Ethan wasn't about to back down now. Something was happening in this town, and he wasn't going to let it slide.

Before he could respond, the stranger who had spoken earlier slid out of his booth and headed for the door. He paused just long enough to meet Ethan's eyes, a knowing look on his face. Ethan's stomach tightened.

"I warned you," the man muttered, his voice low. "They'll make sure you disappear. And you'll never be heard from again."

Ethan felt a chill run down his spine. It wasn't just paranoia. Something was happening here, something far bigger than a simple murder. And the deeper he dug, the more he realized that he was already trapped in a game he hadn't fully understood.

Westfall had secrets. And as Ethan stared at Felicity, he realized that she might hold the key to uncovering them—or becoming a pawn in a game he couldn't yet see. There and then decided to get to know her and access more from her knowledge of what is before him to unravel.

Three

Faded Records

Ethan could feel the cold fingers of unease creeping down his spine as he walked into the Westfall Police Department, the eerie silence of the town still hanging over him. The diner had been little more than a dead end. The waitress hadn't offered anything of value, and the strange man in the booth had simply warned him off, but said nothing that hinted at the truth. But the feeling in his gut told him there was something here, something hidden beneath the surface, waiting to be uncovered.

The police station was no better. The small, dilapidated building stood on the corner of a forgotten street, its windows covered with grime. The inside was just as bleak, with old wood paneling, fluorescent lights flickering above, and walls covered in outdated paperwork. The atmosphere was thick with the weight of years of neglect. If a major crime had ever occurred here, it seemed like no one had bothered to follow up on it.

Faded Records

Ethan approached the front desk, where a sheriff's deputy sat, his face expressionless as he stared at a screen in front of him. The man barely glanced up as Ethan made his way over.

"Can I help you?" the deputy muttered, his tone lacking any real interest.

"I'm looking for old case files," Ethan said, trying to keep his voice steady. "About a year ago, maybe two. A homicide—possibly connected to a missing person."

The deputy's eyes flicked up for a second before returning to the screen. "Homicides in Westfall? That's a rare thing. You'll be wasting your time."

"I'm not wasting anything," Ethan replied, pushing forward. "I need to see what you've got."

The deputy seemed to weigh the request, his fingers tapping idly on the edge of his desk. After a moment, he grunted and pointed to a door behind him. "The archives are in there. Knock yourself out. I've got nothing better to do."

Ethan thanked him curtly and pushed through the door into the back room. Inside, the smell of mildew and old paper hit him, and the sight of rows of filing cabinets stretching from floor to ceiling did little to lift his spirits. The room was stuffy, as if it hadn't seen fresh air in years. He moved past stacks of unorganized boxes and toward a row of cabinets labeled "Closed Cases." A cold chill crept into the back of his mind. It was too quiet, too deliberate. He couldn't shake the feeling that someone was watching him.

He scanned the files for anything that might match the crime scene in the photo—the eerie image that had brought him to Westfall in the first place. His fingers skimmed over the dusty file labels, pausing at a name he found familiar. There it was: "Catherine Weber – Missing Person – Case No. 1987-32." It was a long shot, but it matched the approximate timeframe of the photo's subject. Catherine Weber... the woman in the photo might be someone who had vanished, someone erased by time or manipulation.

He yanked open the drawer, the metal squealing in protest. He thumbed through the file, but what he found made his stomach tighten with dread. The case file was incomplete. The details were scarce. The more he flipped through it, the more disjointed it seemed. There were no statements from witnesses, no information on suspects, and no photographs of the missing woman. Just a single, cryptic note: *"Investigation suspended – No further action required."*

A sense of dread washed over him, and his pulse quickened. How could this be? A missing person's case, one that had apparently been wiped clean. He felt the first true crack in his belief that this was a simple small-town investigation. Something darker was going on.

Ethan slammed the file shut and moved on to the next drawer. His fingers were trembling now, each new case seeming more bizarre than the last. *Another disappearance, another unsolved murder.* But as he pulled file after file, it was the same story. Wiped clean, blank spaces, missing records. A town that was clearly hiding something.

He pulled a file out of the last drawer, his breath catching in his throat. This one wasn't like the others. The case number stood out: *"Murder – Unsolved – Case No. 2004-91."* The details inside were sparse, but one thing was immediately apparent: this case had been closed without a resolution. What caught his attention was the name of the victim: *Matthew Reese*. The photo... He recognized the name. Reese was one of the faces in the crime scene photo. The blurred figure. The one who had

Faded Records

been... erased from history.

Suddenly, the hairs on the back of his neck stood up. His eyes raced across the file, but there was nothing—no evidence, no photos, no trail of leads. The only thing that seemed to have been preserved was a name—a name he recognized all too well. The file's notation read, *"Investigation closed – No further action."*

He grabbed the file, his mind racing as he tried to make sense of the chaos. Who would do this? Who had the power to wipe out entire histories, to erase people from the records of time? It was clear that someone was manipulating the facts, shaping the past to suit a purpose he couldn't yet understand. But what purpose? And how far did this conspiracy reach?

Before he could dwell on the thought, a voice behind him broke his concentration.

"You're not supposed to be here."

Ethan froze, the voice cutting through the silence like a blade. Slowly, he turned to see a man standing in the doorway, his arms crossed. He was tall, dressed in a suit that looked too expensive for a town like Westfall. His face was a mask of indifference, but there was something in his eyes that hinted at a deeper knowledge. A man who had seen too much.

"I'm just looking for some information," Ethan said, his voice low. He didn't like where this was going. The man was no ordinary officer. He knew too much.

"Looking for information?" The man took a step closer, his gaze never leaving Ethan. "You won't find it here. Not anymore."

Ethan clenched his jaw, feeling his gut twist. "Who are you?"

The man didn't answer directly. Instead, he stepped further into the room, his gaze flicking to the file in Ethan's hand. His eyes narrowed slightly. "The question is, why are you looking?"

Ethan didn't trust him. There was something off about him—a presence that was too controlled, too calculating. He instinctively reached for his phone, ready to call Samira, but the man was quick. He moved in a blur, blocking Ethan's path before he could dial.

"Think very carefully about what you're doing," the man said, his voice like velvet. "You're digging up things that were never meant to be found."

Ethan's instincts screamed at him to leave—to get out of this suffocating room and back to safety. But he couldn't. Not now. Not when the pieces were starting to come together. He couldn't let this man intimidate him. Not when he was so close to the truth.

"I don't know who you are, but I'm not stopping," Ethan said, staring the man down.

The man's lips curled into a tight smile, almost pitying. "Then I guess you'll see for yourself."

And with that, the man turned and walked out of the room, leaving Ethan alone in the silence once more.

As the door clicked shut behind him, Ethan's mind raced. The cases, the disappearances, the strange man—everything was beginning to fit into a pattern. But the more he uncovered, the more disorienting it became. This wasn't just about a murder that hadn't happened. It was about control. About erasing people, erasing facts, and rewriting history itself.

And for the first time, Ethan wasn't sure whether he was investigating a crime—or becoming part of the cover-up.

The eerie silence of the town hung in the air as he left the police station, the sense of something terrible brewing growing stronger with every step. He needed answers. And he had a feeling that the deeper he dug, the more the world around him would unravel.

One thing was for sure: nothing was as it seemed in Westfall, and the truth he was chasing would cost him far more than he had anticipated.

Four

The Revisionists

The air in the back of the abandoned warehouse was thick with dust and dampness, the kind of oppressive weight that made it hard to breathe. Ethan stood in the shadows, the creak of his boots muffled against the uneven concrete floor. His mind was racing, and his instincts were on high alert. He had stumbled into something—something big. But what? His gut twisted with the sense that the answer was close, but just out of reach.

He'd followed the trail of oddities for days: the strange disappearances, the erased records, the disjointed fragments of memories that didn't align with reality. But it wasn't until now, standing in front of this locked door—one he was certain was meant to keep people like him out—that the enormity of it all hit him.

The Revisionists.

A name that had slipped from one of his old informants,

a name he had thought was a rumor, a whispered legend in underground circles. But the more Ethan pieced together, the clearer it became that The Revisionists were not just a conspiracy theory—they were real. And their power, their reach, was far beyond anything he had imagined.

As he fumbled with the lock, a strange, almost electric hum filled the air. His pulse quickened, and he pushed the door open with a creak, stepping into the room beyond. The low buzz intensified, and his breath caught in his throat.

Rows of monitors lined the walls, some flickering with static, others displaying cryptic data. The place was a high-tech hub, a far cry from the decaying building he had expected. The dim blue light from the screens cast long, eerie shadows across the space, and for a moment, Ethan felt like he had stumbled upon a hidden world—a world that had been carefully constructed and guarded for far too long.

He reached for the nearest terminal, glancing around quickly. No one appeared to be present, but his instincts told him to be cautious. He keyed in a simple code he had managed to procure from a confidential source, one that had been hesitant to give up any useful information, but had spilled a few cryptic words before disappearing. The screen blinked to life, and Ethan's breath caught. There, on the monitor, was a name: *The Revisionists.*

The text was buried in a directory labeled *Advanced Security Protocols*—a strange name for a group of people, but it made sense given what Ethan had uncovered about their operations. The page was sparse, but enough was visible to send a chill through his spine.

The Revisionists were an organization of elite individuals, some operating from the shadows, some in plain sight. They were not interested in money, or power in the traditional sense. Their goal, according to the cryptic text, was far more insidious: to rewrite history itself.

They had access to some of the most advanced technologies on the planet—technology capable of altering not only criminal records but memories, events, and, it seemed, entire histories. It was almost too much to comprehend, but the implications were impossible to ignore. The Revisionists controlled what people remembered, what they saw, what they believed. Their influence over the truth was absolute.

Ethan's heart pounded as the pieces started to come together. The erased records, the missing people, the changes in reality that felt too deliberate to be coincidence. It was all tied to The Revisionists—and their ability to manipulate history itself.

He scrolled further, hoping for more, but the screen abruptly went dark. A jolt of panic ran through him. The humming sound grew louder, and a voice crackled through the speakers above.

"You shouldn't have come here."

Ethan spun around, his eyes darting to the entrance of the room. A tall, imposing figure stepped forward from the shadows, a man who appeared to materialize out of thin air. His face was masked, his posture rigid and confident. Ethan's instincts screamed danger, but he forced himself to stay calm.

"I'm not here to cause trouble," Ethan said, his voice steady despite the tension tightening in his chest. "I'm just trying to understand what's going on. People are disappearing. Cases are being erased. This isn't a coincidence."

The man tilted his head, his voice low and smooth as it reverberated in the room. "You think you understand, but you don't. There's more at stake here than you could ever imagine.

History is fragile. If the wrong hands control it, everything you believe in can be altered in an instant. Everything you hold true can be rewritten."

Ethan narrowed his eyes. "Who are you?"

The figure hesitated, his mask twitching as if it were contemplating whether to reveal the truth. "We are The Revisionists. And we've been watching you, Ethan Voss. Your search for the truth has brought you to the edge of something far larger than you realize."

Ethan's breath caught. He had heard rumors, but hearing it from the mouth of someone involved sent a wave of dread through him. But there was something else, too—something familiar in the man's tone, like a distant echo of a memory he couldn't quite place.

"The truth about the disappearances. About the history that's been erased," the figure continued. "It's all part of a larger plan. A plan we've been carefully crafting for years."

Ethan's mind was spinning, but one question burned through the fog of confusion. "What does Carter Langston have to do with all of this?"

At the mention of the name, the figure stiffened. For a moment, Ethan thought he saw a flicker of recognition in the man's eyes—something telling him that the connection was more than just coincidental.

"Langston?" The figure's voice was harder now, almost cold. "You don't understand. He's one of us, but his involvement is more… complicated. Voryx Technologies is the key. They control the AI that powers much of what we do. But Langston has always been more… ambitious than we originally intended."

Ethan's heart skipped a beat. Voryx Technologies. The cutting-edge AI company based in New York. The same company owned by Carter Langston. A company that had access to some of the most advanced technology in the world. And if what the man was saying was true, then Voryx had somehow become the backbone of The Revisionists' operations.

"What are you saying?" Ethan asked, his voice barely above a whisper.

The figure stepped closer, his face still hidden beneath the mask. "Voryx Technologies, through its AI systems, allows us to manipulate not just information, but reality itself. Langston's company provided the technology that enabled us to rewrite memories, erase people from existence, alter the very fabric of history."

Ethan staggered back, his mind reeling. "You're saying Voryx is behind all of this? That Langston's company is responsible for the disappearances? For the murders that haven't even happened yet?"

The figure nodded slowly. "Langston's ambition has always exceeded our expectations. He believes in a new world order—one where the powerful control not just the future, but the past as well. But his desire for control is dangerous. And if left unchecked, it could unravel everything."

Ethan took a deep breath, trying to steady himself. This was bigger than anything he had imagined. Bigger than any conspiracy he had ever uncovered. He had walked into a storm, and now it seemed like there was no way out. The Revisionists, Langston, Voryx Technologies—everything was connected. The strings were all pulling in one direction, and Ethan was caught in the middle.

"Where do I go from here?" Ethan asked, his voice tinged with frustration. "How do I stop this?"

The figure's voice was cold now, almost mocking. "You don't.

You can't. This is bigger than you, Ethan. And the more you dig, the more you'll realize that you're already part of the plan. Welcome to the future."

With that, the figure turned and disappeared into the shadows, leaving Ethan standing alone in the dimly lit room. His mind was spinning, his thoughts racing. The world around him felt like it was collapsing into chaos.

Voryx Technologies. The Revisionists. Carter Langston. It was all connected, and there was no going back now.

Ethan's only choice was to keep digging. But as he turned to leave the room, he couldn't shake the feeling that the walls were closing in. The truth was out there, but so was something darker, something he had yet to fully understand.

And the closer he got to it, the more he feared he might lose himself along the way.

Five

Felicity's Awakening

Felicity Harris sat at her desk, fingers poised over the sleek keyboard of her laptop, but her mind was elsewhere. The office around her buzzed with the usual rhythm of high-stakes law: ringing phones, whispered conversations, the frantic tapping of keys. But none of it reached her—none of it mattered anymore. She was numb, lost in a sea of doubt that had slowly been sinking her for the past few days.

It had started innocuously enough—subtle. A case, a small discrepancy, a colleague who disappeared for a few days, and then came back as if nothing had happened. But the more she noticed, the more unsettling it became. The absence of records. The vanishing people. The way certain things just didn't add up anymore.

And then there was Ethan Voss.

She had crossed paths with him a couple of weeks earlier at

the dingy diner christened "The Last Stop" in Westfall, a small town nestled in a remote corner of the state when on a visit to her uncle, who lost his wife. And just three days ago, when he had approached her in the firm's lobby, she had brushed him off at first, assuming he was just another investigator chasing a wild theory when they had first met outside the city. But his persistence and the oddness of his inquiries had intrigued her. It wasn't just the case he was working on—it was his quiet intensity, the conviction in his eyes that made her question everything she had ever believed about the law.

She had heard rumors about him, of course. Ethan Voss, the former cop turned private investigator, known for his unorthodox methods and the occasional run-in with the law. He was a man who seemed always just on the edge of breaking some rule or law—and yet, he got results. But that was part of what unsettled her. She had spent her life in a world where rules were sacred, where the law was not just a career but a calling. What would drive a man like Ethan to step outside of those boundaries? And, more chillingly, why did she feel as though she were being pulled into his orbit?

Felicity adjusted her glasses, blinking a few times as if trying to shake off the strange sensation of being watched. She glanced at the clock—8:45 p.m. The office was quiet now. Most of the lawyers and paralegals had gone home for the evening, leaving only a few late-night workers. But there was a tension in the air tonight that was different. It was as if something had shifted, something irreparable, and the firm itself had become a part of it.

She stood up from her desk, the leather of her chair creaking as she pushed it back. She needed air. Space. Maybe then, she could clear her head.

As she made her way toward the elevator, her phone buzzed in her pocket. She pulled it out, half-expecting another trivial message from a colleague, but the name on the screen made her pause. Ethan Voss.

She glanced around the empty office, as though the walls themselves might be listening. Her instincts told her to ignore it, to keep walking, but her fingers betrayed her. She answered.

"Ethan?"

"Felicity," his voice crackled through the phone, laced with a sharp edge that made her pause. "I need your help."

Her stomach twisted, and she instinctively glanced at the elevator, a sense of foreboding creeping in. "I can't help you, Ethan. You know what I do. I work for a firm that deals with—"

"I know what you do," he interrupted, his voice low, urgent. "But this isn't about your firm. It's bigger than that. People are disappearing, Felicity. Not just from your office, but from everywhere. I've seen the evidence, and I know you have, too."

She hesitated, her finger still gripping the phone. How could he know about the oddities she had been noticing? How could he know about the whispers in the corridors? The strange absences, the odd gaps in people's memories?

"What do you mean, disappearing? People don't just vanish, Ethan. This isn't a conspiracy theory."

"No, it's not," he said firmly. "This is real. And I need your help to prove it."

Felicity shook her head, disbelief washing over her. She wanted to laugh, to tell him he had gone off the deep end, but something in his tone made her pause. There was an edge to his voice, something primal that made her question everything she thought she knew. A moment of silence passed between them.

"Look," he continued, "I don't expect you to understand right now. But I've found something. Something that connects your firm to all of this. If you want to know what's really going on, you need to come with me."

A chill ran down her spine, but before she could protest, the line went dead. The sudden quiet on the other end of the call was deafening, and her heart hammered in her chest. Her mind raced. Was this a trap? Had she been played?

But the thought of all the things she had seen—the disappearances, the records erased, the unsettling emptiness of her own life—kept gnawing at her. For the first time in months, doubt crept into her thoughts. Was she really living in the world she thought she was?

Against her better judgment, she found herself heading toward the door. She stepped outside the office building, the cool night air biting at her skin as she walked toward the street. The city was alive with its usual chaos—people rushing home, cars honking, the distant hum of conversation. But it felt hollow. Like she was surrounded by ghosts.

Felicity didn't know what she expected when she arrived at the address Ethan had given her—an old, nondescript building on the outskirts of the city—but she certainly hadn't expected the darkness. The street was empty, the buildings lining the road standing like silent sentinels, blocking the light of the few scattered streetlamps.

She glanced up at the address. It was a simple warehouse, the kind of place she had driven by countless times without giving it a second thought. But now, standing in front of it, she could feel the weight of something ominous pressing down on her chest. She felt like she was being pulled into a dark hole she couldn't escape from, and yet, she couldn't turn back now.

The door creaked as it opened, and she stepped inside.

The first thing she noticed was the smell—old wood, something metallic, like blood. The second thing was the silence. There was no hum of machinery, no noise of people working. Just the sound of her breath, the thudding of her heart in her ears.

Ethan emerged from the shadows, his face haggard, eyes wild with determination.

"Felicity," he greeted her, his voice tinged with a mixture of relief and urgency. "You came."

She swallowed hard, feeling the weight of his words settle over her like a shroud. "What is this place?"

"It's where it all starts," Ethan replied, his gaze flicking nervously to the dim corners of the room. "The Revisionists are real, Felicity. They're the ones behind all the disappearances. Behind everything you've seen."

Felicity felt her stomach turn. She had heard the name before, in passing, a whispered rumor among lawyers and investigators. But she had never taken it seriously. To her, it had been no more than a legend, a story told to scare the naïve.

"Who are they?" she asked, her voice barely above a whisper. "What do they want?"

Ethan stepped forward, his hands trembling. "They want control. They want to rewrite history itself. Erase anyone who stands in their way. They've infiltrated every part of the system—law, government, business. Your firm, Felicity…it's a part of it."

She felt her blood run cold at his words. "No. That's impossible. You're telling me that my entire career—everything I've worked for—is a lie?"

Ethan nodded grimly. "I'm afraid so."

Felicity's mind spun, the pieces of the puzzle falling into place with an eerie finality. This wasn't just a case. It wasn't just a conspiracy. This was a war—a war against the very fabric of reality itself. And somehow, she had become a part of it.

"I don't know if I can do this," she whispered, more to herself than to him. "I'm not like you, Ethan. I don't know how to fight this."

Ethan placed a hand on her shoulder, his grip firm and reassuring. "You don't have to do it alone. We're in this together now."

Felicity nodded, the weight of the decision settling in. She didn't know what the future held, but one thing was certain—there was no turning back.

Six

The Man Who Never Was

The dim light of the streetlamp cast long shadows across the empty alley, its pale glow making the wet pavement shimmer with a dull sheen. Ethan Voss stood at the edge of the sidewalk, waiting, his mind racing with possibilities, each one darker than the last. The night had taken on a sinister weight, and the longer he stood there, the more he felt as though the very world around him was becoming... unhinged.

He glanced at his watch. 10:15 p.m. He had agreed to meet the witness at this hour, when the streets would be quiet and they wouldn't be interrupted. His contact—Paul Strickland—had been reluctant to speak, but after weeks of digging, Ethan had managed to track him down. Strickland was a key witness in the case he was investigating, someone who had been involved with the people in the mysterious photograph, but who had inexplicably vanished in the months since. His appearance tonight was the last chance Ethan had to piece together the growing puzzle, to find the one thread that would unravel the conspiracy he suspected was behind the series of vanished memories, erased identities, and missing people.

But as the minutes ticked by, Ethan's hope began to fade, replaced by the gnawing feeling that something was very wrong.

He heard the soft shuffle of footsteps in the alley behind him, and he turned, his heart skipping a beat. A man emerged from the darkness, his features shrouded beneath the brim of a baseball cap. Ethan couldn't make out his face, but he recognized the figure—the posture, the deliberate movements—as the person he had been waiting for. Paul Strickland.

"Ethan Voss," the man said, his voice low and raspy, as he approached, eyes darting nervously left and right.

"Paul Strickland?" Ethan asked, his voice steady despite the rising tension. He stepped forward and extended his hand, but Strickland only looked at it, then back at him.

"Yeah. That's me," Strickland replied, his voice tight. "I didn't think you'd find me so soon."

Ethan studied him closely. The man looked older than the photos he had seen of him. Strickland's eyes were bloodshot, and his clothes were unkempt, as though he hadn't bothered to change in days. His presence here didn't make sense. Strickland had been off the grid for months, yet here he was, showing up in the middle of the night as if everything was normal.

"I don't have much time," Strickland continued, glancing over his shoulder nervously. "They'll be looking for me. I can't stay long. They... they've already erased me once."

"Erased you?" Ethan repeated, confusion clouding his thoughts. "What do you mean, erased?"

Strickland shuddered visibly, running a hand through his

disheveled hair. "I mean they've taken everything. My job. My records. My apartment. Even my family..." His voice trailed off as if the weight of it was too much to bear. He looked at Ethan with a haunted expression, his lips trembling. "I'm not supposed to exist anymore."

A cold chill crept up Ethan's spine. This was no longer just a case of vanishing people or erased files. Strickland wasn't just hiding from someone—he was a man whose very existence had been wiped away, like a name erased from a ledger. Ethan couldn't understand it, but deep down, he knew Strickland was telling the truth.

"What happened to you?" Ethan pressed, his voice softer now, sensing the man's fragile state.

"I was part of the project," Strickland whispered, eyes darting nervously to the street behind him. "I didn't know at first, but I got too close to something I shouldn't have. A company... Voryx Technologies. Carter Langston's company."

Ethan felt a tightening in his chest at the mention of the name. Voryx Technologies. The AI giant. The same company owned by the billionaire, Carter Langston, the man convicted of mass murder in the previous year. The same company whose technology might be tied to the manipulation of reality itself. Ethan had seen Langston's name come up in his investigation before, but it seemed like too much of a stretch. Yet now, with Strickland's words, the pieces were slowly starting to fit.

"Voryx?" Ethan repeated. "What does Voryx have to do with this? What project were you part of?"

Strickland hesitated, his eyes darting around as though he were expecting someone to leap out from the shadows. The paranoia was palpable, but it was justified. The sense of danger was suffocating.

"They're using AI to... to rewrite reality," Strickland whispered, his voice shaking. "Not just digital records—everything. Memories. People. History itself."

Ethan's stomach churned. He had suspected something like this was going on, but hearing it confirmed was something else entirely. He had thought that maybe, just maybe, the conspiracy was limited to some rogue individuals—or a small, powerful group working in the shadows. But now, it seemed like the manipulation of reality itself was within reach of an entire organization. Voryx wasn't just an AI company—it was a tool for altering the very fabric of the world.

"They've erased me," Strickland continued, his voice barely above a whisper. "The company. Langston's people—they took everything. I've been living in the cracks of the world, but I remember. I remember everything."

Ethan opened his mouth to respond, but before he could say a word, Strickland's eyes widened. He froze, his body stiffening, and his mouth opened as if to speak, but no sound came out. He was staring at something—at someone—just behind Ethan.

Ethan's instincts kicked in. He spun around, his hand reaching for his gun, but there was no one there. Just the alley, empty except for the two of them.

When he turned back, Strickland was gone. Just... gone. As if he had never been there in the first place. There was no trace of him—no footsteps, no sounds of retreating footsteps. Nothing.

Ethan's breath caught in his throat. His mind raced, trying to make sense of what had just happened. One moment, Strickland was standing in front of him, speaking in urgent whispers about the horrors he had witnessed. The next moment, the man had vanished into thin air, leaving no trace behind.

Ethan's heart pounded in his chest as he scanned the alley once more. His hand tightened around his gun, though his logical mind told him there was no one there. He moved forward, step by cautious step, but there was nothing—no sign of struggle, no clue, not even a shift in the air. It was as if Strickland had simply ceased to exist.

For a long moment, Ethan stood frozen, the weight of what had just happened settling over him like a cold, suffocating blanket. He had heard of people vanishing. He had heard the rumors of missing persons and unexplained disappearances. But this? This was something different. This was something far more dangerous. Strickland hadn't just vanished—he had been erased.

Ethan's mind raced as he tried to process it all. Was he being targeted? Was this all part of some twisted game, a test to break him, to make him question his own sanity? Or was reality itself cracking apart, pieces of it vanishing and shifting before his very eyes?

He didn't know, but one thing was certain: this was no longer just a case. This was a battle for something far greater—something that threatened to unravel everything he had ever known.

As the weight of Strickland's disappearance settled into his bones, Ethan turned and made his way back to his car, his mind spinning with more questions than answers. The night had swallowed up his witness, and the world itself seemed just a little more fractured than it had been an hour ago. And yet, Ethan knew one thing with absolute certainty:

He wasn't going to stop. Not now. Not ever.

The truth was out there. And he was going to find it—no matter the cost.

Seven

A Familiar Face

The hum of the fluorescent lights overhead was the only sound in the small, windowless office. Ethan Voss sat hunched over his desk, surrounded by scattered case files, his mind heavy with the weight of the puzzle he was trying to solve. Outside, the city buzzed with its usual rhythm, but inside the cramped, dimly lit space, the world felt oddly distant, as though something fundamental was shifting just out of sight.

Ethan had been at this for hours—no, longer. His eyes burned from staring at the papers in front of him, the text blurring and reforming every few seconds. His mind refused to stay focused, dragging him down strange mental corridors where faces appeared and disappeared like shifting ghosts.

He gripped the edge of the desk, taking a deep breath to clear the fog in his head. He needed to focus. He couldn't afford to let this—whatever this was—distract him. He had a job to do. The case. The disappearing people. The erased memories.

Strickland's cryptic warnings about being "erased."

Stay on track, he thought. *Find the answers.*

Ethan turned back to the pile of files he'd pulled from the archives earlier that day. Each one contained a fragment of the mystery, pieces of a shattered whole he was struggling to assemble. As his eyes scanned the names and dates in front of him, one particular file caught his attention.

The case file was thin—barely a dozen pages—and yet it felt heavier than the others. The name on the cover page sent an unsettling jolt through him: *Thomas Lark.*

The name felt like a pull in the back of his mind, something he should know. Ethan sat back, trying to recall why this name felt so important. He scanned the file's contents: a standard murder case, a missing person report, the usual police procedural notes.

But something about it wasn't right. The more Ethan read, the more the name *Thomas Lark* gnawed at him, as if it were a thread he should pull, but every time he reached for it, it slipped from his grasp.

He flipped through the pages again, his fingers trembling ever so slightly. A police report. A witness statement. A picture of a man—a suspect—standing by a streetlight, looking off to the side as though avoiding the camera. He looked familiar, but Ethan couldn't place him. No, that wasn't the problem. The problem was that Ethan had never seen the man before, and yet the image stirred something deep within him, a memory that didn't quite fit.

I know him, Ethan thought. But how? *Where have I seen him before?*

He stared at the image, his mind suddenly flooded with fragments of memories—snippets of a time that didn't seem to belong to his present life. A group of detectives sitting around a table, laughing. A dark-haired man handing Ethan a folder, his face serious but not unkind. The sound of a door closing, the faint scent of cigarette smoke...

Stop it, Ethan thought. *Focus.*

He closed his eyes for a moment, trying to clear the haze. But the more he tried to shake off the feeling of familiarity, the stronger it became. It was as if he had known this man for years, as if their paths had crossed countless times. But when? Where? And more importantly, why couldn't he remember anything concrete?

The answer came to him slowly, like a whisper threading its way through the fog. The man in the picture—Thomas Lark— was someone Ethan had worked with before. Someone in his past. But he didn't remember him. Ethan's chest tightened. That wasn't possible, was it? How could someone so familiar, so real, be part of his life yet now seem like a ghost?

He reached for his phone, dialing the number he knew all too well. He needed to confirm this. He needed someone to tell him he wasn't losing his mind.

It rang twice before a voice on the other end answered.

"Ethan? Is everything okay?" Samira Cross's voice came through, clear and steady, but tinged with concern.

"I need your help," Ethan said, his voice rough. "I'm looking at a case file—Thomas Lark. It's from... a few years ago, I think. I don't remember working on it. But I know I did. The thing is... I don't remember *him.*"

There was a long pause on the other end, and then Samira spoke. "Ethan, you're going to have to slow down. What do you mean you don't remember him? Was he involved in one of the cases?"

"I don't know. That's the thing. I've never seen this file before, but… I'm looking at the picture of the guy. I know him. I feel like I've known him forever, but I can't recall where from. It's like someone is messing with my memories. This isn't just about the case. It's… *him*."

Samira's voice softened. "Maybe you're just under stress. You've been working nonstop. Take a step back."

"No," Ethan interrupted, his voice sharp. "This isn't stress. Something is wrong. I'm telling you, Samira. This isn't just about the people in the files. This is about me. I'm starting to lose track of who I am. Who I've been."

Silence hung between them, but then Samira spoke again, her voice steady, despite the undertone of concern. "Alright. Let's go over the facts. You're looking at a case file you don't remember working on. You're looking at a man you don't remember meeting. And you're telling me you know him. You feel like you've known him. But the truth is, there's nothing that says you ever did, right?"

"Exactly."

"We need to dig into this Lark case. Maybe it's connected to everything else."

Ethan rubbed his eyes, frustration building. "I don't know, Samira. The more I look at this, the more things don't add up. The more it feels like I'm walking through a dream, a memory that's been twisted. It's all slipping through my fingers."

"Stay with me, Ethan. We'll figure this out. But we can't do it alone."

Ethan knew she was right. He couldn't do this alone. He needed Samira. And he needed more than that. He needed answers.

"Alright. I'll dig deeper into the Lark case. Maybe it'll lead somewhere. Maybe… it'll lead me to whatever is happening to my head."

"I'm here, Ethan. Whatever you need."

As he ended the call, Ethan's gaze drifted back to the photograph of Thomas Lark. The face, the name, everything about it felt like it was part of his life, and yet... it wasn't. He looked again at the officer's notes. They were minimal, outlining the basics of the case: Lark had been a suspect in a string of burglaries and assaults. Nothing special. But the more Ethan thought about it, the more his gut churned. He felt as though he was looking at a man who didn't belong in this case file.

Why can't I remember him?

With a surge of unease, Ethan turned the page, scanning for more details, something that would make sense of the odd feeling gnawing at him. But the next page revealed something even more unsettling: A note in bold red ink: *Case closed. No further investigation needed. Deleted from records.*

Ethan's blood ran cold.

He slammed the file shut, his heart pounding. He knew what that meant. His head was spinning, his breath coming faster. The case, the man, the file—it was all fading. As if someone had erased him from history. Someone had erased Thomas Lark.

"Who are you?" Ethan muttered to the empty room, his voice trembling. He sat back, a sinking feeling gnawing at his stomach. "And why can't I remember you?"

The world felt different now. The people he'd known. The things he'd done. The city that had always been familiar—it was all slipping away. Ethan's memories felt fragile, like they were being overwritten, one by one. He couldn't trust them. Not anymore.

And now, the man who *shouldn't* exist was at the center of it all.

With a sharp breath, Ethan grabbed his coat and stormed out of his office, the door slamming shut behind him. He didn't know where he was going, but he knew he couldn't sit still. He couldn't stay in a world where reality itself was in question.

Not when he didn't even know if he was the one who belonged in it anymore.

Eight

Agent Pierce's Warning

The phone rang, its shrill tone cutting through the heavy silence in Ethan's apartment. He had been sitting in the dim glow of his desk lamp, staring at the same set of files for the better part of an hour, trying to make sense of the jumble of names, dates, and faces that seemed to be slipping through his fingers. His mind was a maze of unanswered questions, and the more he searched for answers, the more the walls seemed to close in.

The ring of the phone sliced through his thoughts, and Ethan's heart skipped a beat. He had been expecting the call for days now, but the truth was, he wasn't sure if he was ready to hear what it had to offer.

He glanced at the caller ID. The number was unlisted. A private number. Only one person had that kind of access to him.

Ethan exhaled sharply and picked up the phone.

"Voss," he said, his voice steady but laced with caution.

A brief silence hung in the air before the voice on the other end spoke, low and deliberate, carrying the unmistakable weight of authority.

"Ethan Voss," the voice said. "I was wondering when you'd pick up."

Ethan's fingers tightened around the receiver. He could feel the coldness creeping up his spine. "Malcolm Pierce," he said, though it wasn't a question. It couldn't be anyone else.

"Glad to know you're still alive," Pierce said, his tone dark, almost amused. "I had my doubts."

"What do you want?" Ethan's voice sharpened. There was a hint of bitterness there, a realization that their tenuous alliance was starting to unravel. Ethan had been playing along for too long, but now things were beginning to feel too dangerous, even for him.

Pierce chuckled, but there was no warmth in it. "I think you know why I'm calling. You've been digging into things you don't understand, Voss. And believe me, you don't want to know what you're getting yourself into."

Ethan's jaw clenched. He leaned forward, elbows resting on the desk, his gaze flicking to the pile of case files spread out before him. "I'm not scared of the truth, Pierce. And I'm damn sure not scared of you."

"You should be," Pierce said, his voice growing cold. "Because the truth, Voss, is a dangerous thing. Especially when you start uncovering things that have been buried for a very long time."

The words hung in the air like a threat, and Ethan could feel a chill creeping through the room. He was beginning to realize how little he knew about the man on the other end of the line. Agent Malcolm Pierce was a shadow, a ghost, someone who had been on the periphery of this entire case for longer than Ethan could have guessed. And Pierce's cryptic warnings only seemed to add to the weight of the mystery pressing in on him.

"Why should I trust you?" Ethan asked, his voice tight with suspicion. "You've been watching me, haven't you? Following me, monitoring my every move. And now you want to give me a warning? About what?"

Pierce's laugh was dry, almost bitter. "Trust, huh? I don't expect you to trust me, Voss. Hell, I'm not asking for it. But I'm offering you something you don't have: perspective. I've been tracking the Revisionists for years. I know what they're capable of. What they've done. And what they're planning to do next."

Ethan's breath caught. The Revisionists. The name had been creeping into his investigation, like a shadow lurking just beyond his reach. He had seen the signs, heard the whispers, but it wasn't until now that the full weight of their power began to settle into place.

"What are they, Pierce? A group of rich elitists pulling strings from behind the curtain? A bunch of crazies with too much power?" Ethan's voice was laced with skepticism.

"There's no easy answer to that," Pierce said, his tone darkening. "They're not just a group of people. They're a system. A system built to rewrite history. And they've been doing it for decades. You've seen the signs—the disappearing people, the erased records, the cases that vanish into thin air. They control information. They manipulate perception. They have the means to alter reality itself. And now, Voss, they've set their sights on you."

Ethan could feel the tension rising in his chest. "What the hell are you talking about? Why me?"

"Because you're digging in places you shouldn't be." Pierce's voice dropped, becoming more intense. "And if you're not careful, you'll end up like all the others. Disappeared. Forgotten. Erased."

Ethan stood abruptly, pacing the length of his apartment as Pierce's words echoed in his mind. "You're telling me I'm going to be erased? Like those people I've been investigating?"

"That's what they do, Voss. That's what the Revisionists do. They take what doesn't fit into their version of the world and make it vanish. History, memories, people—whatever it takes to protect their agenda. They've done it for years, and now they're going after you because you're getting too close to the truth."

Ethan's mind raced. The pieces were starting to fall into place, but they were incomplete. The Revisionists—who were they really? How far did their reach go? And where did he fit into this twisted puzzle?

"I don't know if I can trust you, Pierce," Ethan said, the suspicion in his voice palpable. "You've been hiding in the shadows for years, and now you want to give me advice? I don't need your warnings, and I sure as hell don't need your help."

Pierce's voice softened, but the edge remained. "You're going to need it, whether you like it or not. I've been tracking them for years, Voss. I know how they think. I know their patterns. And you're already in too deep. It's not a matter of *if* they come for you. It's a matter of *when*."

Ethan's chest tightened as he clenched the phone in his hand. He could feel the walls closing in, the pressure mounting, the sense of danger rising with every word Pierce spoke.

"I don't have time for this," Ethan said, his voice a low growl.

Agent Pierce's Warning

"I need answers. Not cryptic warnings."

"You're not going to get them all at once," Pierce replied. "But I'll give you one piece of advice, Voss. There's a woman you need to meet. Her name is Felicity Harris. She's a lawyer, high-profile, sharp as hell. She's been noticing the same things you have—the people disappearing, the records vanishing. She's not yet in as deep as you are, but she's on the right track. She might be your key to getting to the heart of this."

Ethan frowned. "What makes you think I need her help?"

"Because," Pierce said, his tone suddenly more grave, "she's seen the cracks in the system too. She just doesn't know what she's looking at yet. But she will. And when she does, you'll need to be ready."

The line went silent for a moment, and Ethan could hear the faint rustling of papers in the background, the sound of someone shifting in a chair.

"If you're smart," Pierce continued, his voice quieter now, "you'll find her. And you'll work with her. Because, Voss, the Revisionists don't just erase people—they erase everything. Your memories. Your life. Your past. Your future. They rewrite it all. And if you don't stop them, you'll be the next thing they make disappear."

The phone clicked in his ear, and the line went dead. Ethan stood frozen, staring at the receiver in his hand. The words replayed in his mind, over and over, until they became an inescapable drumbeat in his skull.

They erase everything.

And now, it seemed, he was the next one on their list.

Ethan dropped the phone onto the table and walked to the window. The city sprawled out before him, the lights of the buildings twinkling in the distance. He felt small in the face of what he had uncovered, the weight of it pressing on his chest. The Revisionists weren't just a conspiracy. They were a force—powerful, invisible, and ruthless.

And somehow, he had just become their target.

Nine

Shifting Realities

The world was never the same twice.

Ethan stood in front of the coffee machine, staring at the black liquid bubbling up into the carafe. It was early morning, the first light of dawn just starting to creep through the blinds of his apartment. His head ached, a dull, persistent throb that had become his constant companion over the past few days. The case was getting to him—more than he was willing to admit.

He reached for the cup, his hand trembling slightly as he poured the hot liquid. As the coffee splashed into the mug, he couldn't shake the sense that something wasn't right. It was subtle, at first, a feeling deep in his gut that he tried to ignore. But now it was impossible to dismiss.

He picked up the mug and walked to the small table by the window, his eyes scanning the cityscape below. New York was always chaotic, always loud, but today it felt different. The noise felt distant, like it wasn't even happening in the same world as him. The people on the street, the honking cars, the distant hum of sirens—everything felt disconnected, as though his mind was too far removed from reality to truly engage with it.

He sat down and ran a hand through his hair, his thoughts racing. The previous night had been a blur, filled with sleepless hours and frenzied note-taking. He'd gone over every file, every clue, trying to find something—anything—that would tie together the strange disappearances, the vanishing records, and the cryptic phone call from Agent Pierce. But the deeper he dug, the more he realized that the case was unraveling in ways he couldn't control.

And now, there was something else. Something... wrong.

He placed his cup on the table and leaned back in his chair, letting his eyes fall shut. But the moment his eyelids closed, the familiar weight of déjà vu settled over him, a creeping sensation that his life was on the verge of repeating itself.

The noise of the street below became muffled, like he was submerged underwater. He opened his eyes, but the world before him seemed different—slightly out of focus, as though the edges of reality had become blurred, softened. His apartment, which he'd lived in for years, looked unfamiliar. The old photo of his mother, the one he'd framed years ago, hung on the wall, but it wasn't where it was supposed to be. His mind recoiled at the change. Had he moved it? No, he would have remembered that.

Shaking his head, he got up, his body moving automatically toward the kitchen. He needed to clear his head, to figure out what was happening to him. He tried to focus on the sound of his footsteps on the hardwood floor, but the rhythm of his walk felt wrong, almost too slow, as if his movements weren't his own.

When he reached the counter, he froze.

There, on the counter, was a picture. It wasn't his—he had no memory of taking it, no recollection of even seeing it before. A photo of a man, standing alone in a crowd, his face blurry and indistinct. But something about it tugged at Ethan's memory. It felt like an echo, like he had seen this image before but couldn't place where. He turned the picture over and saw the words scrawled in a familiar handwriting:

"Don't trust them."

His heart pounded in his chest. Who had left this here? He didn't remember anyone coming into his apartment. He hadn't even opened the door to anyone in days. And yet, this photo was here, as if it had always been part of his life.

Suddenly, the air around him felt thick, suffocating. He reached for his phone, desperate to call Samira, to get her opinion on the photo. But when he unlocked the screen, the device seemed to glitch, the icons flickering and jumping around in a way that made him pause.

He tried calling her anyway.

The line rang for a few moments before it clicked. But instead of hearing Samira's voice, a cold, unfamiliar tone echoed through the phone.

"Ethan... is this real?" the voice said.

His blood ran cold. It wasn't Samira. It wasn't anyone he recognized.

"Who is this?" he demanded, his voice shaky. "Who the hell is this?"

The line went dead.

Ethan dropped the phone onto the table and spun around.

His breath came in shallow gasps, his hands trembling. The walls of his apartment seemed to stretch and contract, like the very space around him was shifting. It was as if he had stepped into someone else's life, and everything he thought he knew was slipping away.

He grabbed the keys to his car and left the apartment, the cold night air hitting his face like a slap. The streets of New York were still buzzing with life, but it felt like they existed in a parallel dimension, like he was just an observer in a world that didn't belong to him.

He drove aimlessly, unable to shake the feeling that the world around him was slipping through his fingers, like sand in an hourglass. He needed answers. He needed something solid to hold onto.

After a while, his car came to a stop in front of a familiar building. It was the police station in Brooklyn, where he had worked years ago, back when he was still a cop. He'd solved countless cases here, some small, some big, but all of them had been tied together by a single truth: justice. He had always believed that if you worked hard enough, you could find the truth.

But as he stepped out of the car and walked toward the entrance, he felt the walls of the building seem to shift, as though it were no longer the place he remembered. The door was ajar, the faint sound of murmured voices coming from inside.

He pushed it open, and the first thing he noticed was the thick layer of dust on the floor, the abandoned desks, and the empty hallways. The lights flickered overhead, casting long shadows that stretched out of reach. The air smelled stale, as if it hadn't been disturbed in years.

He moved cautiously through the building, his footsteps echoing in the hollow silence. He made his way to the records room, where he had spent so many late nights going through case files, trying to make sense of the chaos of crime. But when he reached the door, he hesitated. The file room, too, felt different.

Ethan stepped inside and froze.

The files were gone. Every single one of them. Empty cabinets stood like ghosts in the room, their once organized rows now reduced to nothing but bare metal. He opened drawers, pulling at the handles desperately, but it was useless. The cases he had worked on, the people he had fought to protect, were no longer here.

His mind raced, and for a moment, he couldn't breathe. The room was closing in on him, the walls pressing tighter and tighter. He backed away slowly, stumbling, before he reached the door. He turned around, desperate for a sense of reality, but everything was beginning to blur. The old records, the files, the memories—they were fading.

And then, in the distance, he saw it.

A figure. A silhouette. Standing in the doorway.

It was a person, but the face was too blurred, too distorted to make out. They didn't move. They just stood there, watching him.

Ethan's heart pounded in his chest, his breath shallow as he stumbled backward. The figure didn't speak, but he could feel their eyes on him, cold and unblinking.

He turned and ran, bursting out of the room and into the hallway, the echo of his footsteps trailing behind him. But the hallways seemed to stretch on forever, each turn leading him deeper into a maze he couldn't escape.

Reality was cracking, shattering around him, and there was no place left to hide.

The world was no longer the world he knew.

And he wasn't sure if he could trust his own mind anymore.

Ten

The Vanishing Victim

Ethan Voss's mind raced as he stood outside the crumbling building, the wind biting at his face, making his jacket flap against his chest. He'd spent the past few days trying to connect the dots—figuring out how the missing people, the erased memories, and the cryptic messages were all connected. The case had twisted, bent, and twisted again until it no longer resembled anything he'd ever worked on. But this… this felt different. More dangerous.

The address he'd followed led him to an abandoned warehouse on the edge of the city, tucked away in a forgotten industrial district. The building was old, the kind that looked like it should have been condemned years ago, but there was something about it. The walls, covered in peeling paint and graffiti, didn't speak of neglect. They whispered of secrets.

As he approached the door, his pulse quickened. He hadn't shared this lead with anyone—Samira, Felicity, or even Agent

Pierce. It was too risky. His every instinct screamed at him to turn back, but he knew that the truth, whatever it was, lay inside. And the deeper he got, the closer he would be to understanding the twisted force that had been manipulating his life.

He pressed his ear to the door, listening for sounds. For a moment, there was nothing—just the low hum of the city beyond. Then, faintly, he heard voices. Low, guttural murmurs that seemed to echo from deep within. Ethan's hand hovered over the knob, and with a final glance over his shoulder, he turned it, stepping into the darkness.

The inside of the warehouse smelled of mildew and rust, the air heavy with the scent of damp concrete and decay. Ethan's flashlight cut through the dark, revealing rows of metal filing cabinets, some open, some half-closed. The shadows shifted around him, casting eerie shapes on the walls. It was a graveyard of secrets—each cabinet, each drawer, holding something buried that was never meant to see the light of day.

He moved carefully, his footsteps soft against the floor. He had no idea who—or what—was waiting for him here, but he knew it wasn't going to be good.

As he ventured deeper, the murmurs grew louder. They were not human voices—not in the way he was used to hearing. There was something off about them, like they were too… controlled. Too perfect.

Finally, he reached the back of the warehouse. A door stood ajar, a dim light spilling from the crack. With his gun in hand, he pushed it open slowly.

Inside was a stark contrast to the darkness outside. The room was lit by harsh fluorescent lights, and a long, polished table ran the length of the room. There were men and women seated at it, but none of them were talking. They just stared straight ahead, as though they were waiting for something—or someone. At the far end of the table sat a figure who radiated authority, a man whose mere presence seemed to command the room. His sharp suit and cold eyes gave him away instantly. This was no ordinary person. This was one of them—the Revisionists.

Ethan's heart began to race. He didn't know who this man was, but he could sense the power he held. The entire atmosphere in the room felt stifling, as if every breath was a calculated movement in a game no one could win.

He crept closer, staying in the shadows. His breath quickened when he caught sight of the faces at the table. There was something strange about them—too perfect, too still, as if they were mannequins instead of real people. One face caught his attention: a woman with dark brown hair, pale skin, and a pair of wide eyes that stared into the distance. Something about her looked familiar.

Before he could react, a voice broke the silence.

"Ethan Voss," the man at the end of the table said. "We've been expecting you."

Ethan's blood ran cold. He had been careful—too careful, perhaps. He hadn't expected anyone to know he was coming. But then, he remembered the call he'd received from Agent Pierce the day before. He had warned him that the Revisionists had eyes everywhere.

"Who are you?" Ethan demanded, keeping his voice low but firm. "What is this place?"

The man smiled, a cold, practiced gesture that didn't reach his eyes. "You've been investigating something you don't fully understand, Mr. Voss. We've been keeping an eye on you for a while now. You're not the first to ask these questions. But I must tell you, curiosity has its price."

Ethan's grip on his gun tightened, but he didn't draw it. Not yet.

"Curiosity?" Ethan scoffed. "I think it's more than that. You've been erasing people—erasing memories, rewriting history. Who are you really? What are you trying to hide?"

The man leaned forward, his cold smile never faltering. "You have no idea how much power we wield, Mr. Voss. The truth is a delicate thing. It needs to be… adjusted from time to time. And those who cannot accept that… well, they don't last long."

Ethan's stomach churned, but he didn't back down. "You think you can erase the truth? Rewrite people's lives? You're playing with something you can't control."

The man's smile vanished, and he nodded toward one of the figures seated at the table. The woman with the dark brown hair.

"Take a good look at her," the man said, his voice turning ice cold. "You've met her before. In fact, you've been investigating her death."

Ethan's blood turned to ice.

The woman. The face he had seen in the crime scene photo. The one who had been blurred, distorted, a person who hadn't existed—until now.

Ethan's heart slammed against his ribs as he realized the truth.

The woman at the table wasn't dead. She was alive, sitting right there in front of him, staring at him with those wide, unblinking eyes. But that wasn't what terrified him the most.

It was the fact that she wasn't supposed to be here. She shouldn't even exist, not according to the records. The case he had investigated, the murder, everything—was a lie. She was a lie.

His mind raced. The Revisionists had not only erased her

death—they had erased her entire existence. But why? Why would they do that?

"You... you're alive?" Ethan choked out, his voice barely a whisper.

The woman didn't respond. She didn't even blink.

"She's not the only one," the man said. "There are many others, Ethan. People who have been erased—changed—given new lives. Do you understand now? You're not dealing with a simple case of missing persons. You're dealing with the manipulation of reality itself."

Ethan's head spun. This wasn't just about the erased files or missing witnesses. It was about something far darker, something more insidious. The Revisionists weren't just erasing people—they were rewriting the very fabric of reality, bending it to their will. And if they could do this to people, what else could they do?

He stepped back, his hand shaking as he reached for his phone. He had to warn Samira. Felicity. He had to get out of there before it was too late.

But as he turned to leave, the door slammed shut behind him, and the lights flickered, plunging the room into darkness.

The woman's voice, low and haunting, echoed in the silence.

"You shouldn't have come here, Ethan."

The world around him began to spin, and for a moment, he wasn't sure where he was. The walls seemed to close in on him. The faces at the table were no longer still—they were moving, shifting, distorting like figures from a nightmare.

And as his vision blurred, Ethan realized something even more terrifying.

The Revisionists weren't just controlling history. They were controlling his mind.

Eleven

Echoes of the Past

Ethan's fingers trembled as he stared at the phone screen, the name in the contact list haunting him like an old ghost. He hadn't spoken to Matt Garrett in years. Not since the case that had nearly destroyed them both. Not since that night, when the truth had slipped through their fingers like sand, and they'd both been left with nothing but shadows.

Matt had been more than a partner—he'd been a friend. A confidant. Someone Ethan had trusted with his life. But after the case, everything changed. Matt had disappeared from Ethan's life as if he had never existed, and now, standing on the edge of a breaking point, Ethan was wondering if Matt had ever truly been real.

His thumb hovered over the call button for a moment longer, then he pressed it. The dial tone felt like an eternity, each second stretching longer than the last. When Matt finally picked up, the voice on the other end was distant, unfamiliar.

"Hello?"

Ethan's heart skipped a beat. It was Matt's voice, but something about it sounded... off. There was an emptiness there, a hollowness that had never been there before.

"Matt?" Ethan's voice came out strained, a knot tightening in his chest. "It's Ethan Voss. We worked together a few years ago... on the Warren case."

There was a long pause. Too long.

"Warren case?" Matt's voice was confused, distant. "I... I don't know what you're talking about."

Ethan's stomach sank, his fingers tightening around the phone. "Don't play games with me, Matt. You know exactly what I'm talking about. The missing girl. The bloodstains that led nowhere. The whole thing was covered up, but we both knew what we saw. You don't remember?"

"No," Matt replied flatly, his tone still devoid of recognition. "I... I don't remember anything about a Warren case. Are you sure you've got the right person?"

Ethan felt his head spin. His breath quickened. This wasn't possible. They had been in this together. Matt had been there. They had tracked the evidence, confronted the dead ends, and stared at the walls of silence that no one would ever tear down. He remembered it all so vividly. But now, Matt... Matt didn't even recognize the case. Didn't recognize him.

"Matt, listen to me," Ethan pressed, his voice sharp, insistent. "We were partners on that case. We nearly lost everything because of it. You remember the disappearances, don't you? The... the bodies that never turned up? The witnesses who vanished?"

"Ethan, I don't know what's going on, but I think you're mistaken. I don't have any record of any case like that. And I don't… I don't know you."

The words hit Ethan like a punch in the gut. He stumbled back, leaning against the nearest wall for support. This was impossible. This wasn't how it was supposed to be. He could still hear Matt's voice in his head—the same way it had sounded when they had worked side by side, hunting down the truth. And yet… it was as if that version of Matt had never existed.

Ethan's mind raced. Was this some kind of cruel joke? Or had something even more sinister taken place? Was he the one losing his grip on reality? Had the world around him begun to rewrite itself, erasing the past, erasing people, erasing… him?

"Matt, please," Ethan choked out, his voice breaking. "I need you to tell me the truth. What the hell is going on?"

"I told you," Matt said, the confusion in his voice escalating, "I don't know what you're talking about. But this is getting weird. I'm hanging up now."

Before Ethan could respond, the line went dead.

He stood there for a long moment, the phone still pressed to his ear, listening to the dead silence on the other end. His heartbeat thudded in his chest, his thoughts spinning out of control. He felt like he was suffocating in this nightmare of his own making. How could Matt not remember? How could the case just… vanish from both of their lives?

Ethan's fingers numbly scrolled through his contact list. He tried calling Matt again, but the call went straight to voicemail.

Panic crept in. Something was wrong. He could feel it, deep in his bones. His body, his mind—nothing felt right anymore. He couldn't tell what was real and what was a lie. He was beginning to doubt his own memories. And what's worse… was he the one being erased? Or was it the world around him?

With shaking hands, he pulled up the file on his laptop, trying to find any trace of the Warren case. There had to be something. A file. A report. A photo. But when he opened the folder, he was met with an empty screen. No file. No record. Nothing.

His breath caught in his throat as he navigated through the rest of his saved files. The cases, the interviews, the evidence—it was all gone. Wiped clean. Like it had never existed.

"No..." he whispered, the word barely audible. "No, no, no."

He slammed his hand against the desk, frustration boiling over. This couldn't be happening. He couldn't be losing everything like this. It wasn't just Matt. It wasn't just the case. It was everything. The world he knew—the world he had fought for—was slipping through his fingers like sand.

Ethan closed his eyes, trying to steady himself, trying to make sense of it all. What was he missing? What was happening to him? The people, the places, the cases—none of it made sense anymore. But in the silence of his office, one question lingered in his mind like an insidious whisper:

Had he been erased, or was this just the beginning of something far worse?

The door to his office creaked, pulling him from his thoughts. He turned, startled, and found himself staring at Felicity Harris. She stood in the doorway, her expression one of concern mixed with suspicion.

"Ethan?" she said softly, stepping into the room. "You look like you've seen a ghost."

He rubbed his forehead, his hand shaking. "You wouldn't believe me if I told you."

Felicity raised an eyebrow, but there was something in her eyes—an understanding that had not been there before. "Try me."

Ethan let out a long breath, leaning back in his chair. "I

just spoke to Matt Garrett. He doesn't remember the case we worked on together. The one that got us both… burned. He doesn't even remember me. And when I tried to pull up any files on the case…" He gestured at the empty screen. "It's all gone. Like it never existed."

Felicity's eyes widened, her lips parting slightly. "What the hell are you talking about? You're sure?"

"I'm sure," he said, his voice hollow. "And the worst part is… I don't know if it's me. I don't know if I'm losing my mind or if the world itself is changing."

She stepped closer, her brow furrowing. "This is exactly what you were afraid of, isn't it? The people being erased, the records being erased. The Revisionists. They're behind all of this."

Ethan nodded, unable to deny it. The pieces were starting to fit together, but the more he uncovered, the more twisted the picture became. He'd thought he was investigating a single case. But this? This was something far bigger. Something darker.

And he was only scratching the surface.

"We need to get to the bottom of this," Felicity said, her voice low but firm. "Before it's too late. Before they erase us, too."

Ethan looked at her, his eyes heavy with the weight of his realization. "I don't know if we have much time left."

As he glanced out the window, watching the last of the sunlight disappear behind the buildings, he knew that whatever was happening, whatever was behind the vanishing victims and the shifting realities, it was bigger than anything he had ever faced. And it was coming for him.

Twelve

The Missing Trial

The dim glow of the desk lamp cast long shadows across Ethan's cluttered office. He leaned back in his chair, his gaze fixed on the stack of files spread out before him. A cold cup of coffee sat untouched by his elbow, forgotten hours ago when his mind had become too preoccupied with the revelations that had begun to surface. The walls of his world were closing in, and each new discovery left him with more questions than answers. But this latest one… this one had the potential to tear everything he thought he knew about the system apart.

The trial. The one that didn't exist.

He'd started with a simple lead—a whispered name, a forgotten case number that had slipped through the cracks of history. But as he traced it down, a pattern emerged, one that sent chills creeping up his spine. According to the records, there had been no such trial. Not anywhere. No court transcripts, no press coverage, no mention in any legal databases. It was as though the entire proceeding had been erased from existence. A trial that had never been held, a case that had never been fought.

But Ethan wasn't convinced. The more he dug, the more he uncovered, and it became clear that someone had gone to great lengths to hide the truth. Hidden behind layers of bureaucracy, encrypted files, and erased records was something far more insidious than a single lost trial. This was about control. About shaping reality.

The pieces started to fall into place as Ethan connected the dots. The trial, which was supposedly never held, was linked to a series of high-profile political figures. Some of the names were familiar—wealthy tycoons, politicians with decades of influence, and even a few law enforcement officials. But there were others—more obscure individuals—whose involvement in the trial raised even more questions. Why would such powerful figures be involved in a trial that no one seemed to remember? What were they trying to hide?

The connection to The Revisionists became increasingly undeniable.

He tapped his fingers against the desk, the rhythmic sound almost hypnotic, as he examined the forensic evidence that had somehow survived the purge. A set of blood-stained documents, a photograph of a courtroom filled with shadowed faces, and a single cryptic note that seemed to tie everything back to Voryx Technologies. The AI company had been a name that had floated through the investigation in whispers, always just out of reach. But now it was clear that they were part of the larger conspiracy. The deeper Ethan dug, the more he realized that The Revisionists weren't just altering records—they were rewriting history itself.

The Missing Trial

He closed his eyes, trying to focus. He needed to make sense of all of this, to understand how the pieces fit together. But his mind was heavy with doubts. Every turn seemed to lead him deeper into a labyrinth of lies and manipulation. And now, the missing trial—what was it that The Revisionists didn't want the world to see? What had been hidden from the public eye, erased from existence?

A knock on the door jolted him out of his thoughts. He stood quickly, smoothing his wrinkled shirt as he made his way to the door. When he opened it, Felicity stood in the doorway, her face taut with concern.

"You look like you haven't slept in days," she said, her voice tinged with worry.

"I haven't," Ethan replied, stepping aside to let her in. "And I don't think I will until I figure this out."

Felicity glanced at the pile of files on his desk, her expression hardening as she took in the sight of the scattered evidence. "What are you working on now?"

"The missing trial," Ethan said, his voice low as he gestured to the papers. "It never happened, but somehow it's tied to a bunch of high-profile figures, and everything about it's been erased. I'm starting to think it's not just one case, Felicity. It's much bigger."

Felicity pulled up a chair and sat down, her eyes scanning the documents. "How big are we talking here?"

"Big enough that I think it's not just about erasing crimes," Ethan replied, his voice tense. "It's about controlling entire legal systems. If they can erase this trial, who's to say how many others they've manipulated? How many others they've hidden?"

Felicity looked up at him, her brow furrowed. "You're saying they've been tampering with the law for years?"

Ethan nodded slowly, a chill creeping up his spine. "Not just tampering. Controlling. The Revisionists have their hands in everything—from the courtrooms to the police force, from the media to the political system. They've been erasing the truth and rewriting it as they see fit."

Felicity shook her head in disbelief. "But that's insane. How can they have that much power?"

"I don't know," Ethan said, his voice grim. "But I'm starting to think that Voryx Technologies is part of it. The AI. The way they're able to manipulate records, alter data, change perceptions... it's all connected."

"Voryx?" Felicity repeated, her expression sharpening. "The AI company?"

"The same one," Ethan confirmed. "I've been looking into them for a while now. They've been quietly building something that could change the entire course of history. And I think The Revisionists have found a way to use it."

Felicity's eyes narrowed as she stared at the pile of evidence on the desk. "This... this doesn't make sense. How do you know it's them? How do you know it's Voryx behind all of this?"

Ethan hesitated for a moment, unsure how much to reveal. But something in Felicity's eyes told him that if anyone could help him untangle this mess, it was her. She had the same determination in her eyes that he had once possessed, the same refusal to back down when the truth was at stake.

"I've been digging through the forensic evidence," Ethan said, tapping a set of photographs with his finger. "One of the documents that survived the purge—this set of blood-stained pages—came from the trial. It was part of the evidence in the case, but it's been completely erased. And then there's the photograph of the courtroom. It's not clear who's in the photo, but if you look closely, you can see the Voryx logo in the background."

Felicity leaned forward, examining the photo carefully. She remained silent for a long moment, her eyes scanning the image for any detail she might have missed. "So you think Voryx is helping The Revisionists manipulate the courts?"

"I think they're helping them rewrite history itself," Ethan said, his voice low and urgent. "If they can control the narrative, if they can change what people remember, they can control everything. The legal system, the media, the political landscape—it's all part of the same system. And it's all being manipulated."

Felicity sat back, digesting the information. "But why? What's their endgame?"

"That's what I'm trying to figure out," Ethan said. "What's their motive? And why did they go through so much trouble to erase this trial?"

Felicity let out a slow breath, her eyes distant. "If they can erase the trial, Ethan, they can erase anything. And if they control the courts, they control the people who sit in judgment."

Ethan's thoughts raced. If the Revisionists had this kind of power, it wasn't just about controlling the legal system anymore. It was about controlling reality itself. How many trials had they erased? How many lives had they rewritten?

Felicity stood up, her face hardening. "We need to take this to the authorities. To someone who can actually do something about it."

Ethan shook his head, frustration flooding through him. "I don't think we can trust the authorities anymore. What if they're already compromised? What if they're part of the system?"

She looked at him, a slight frown creasing her forehead. "Then what are we supposed to do? Just keep digging in the dark?"

Ethan paused, his gaze distant as he stared at the stack of evidence. He had no easy answers. But one thing was certain—if he didn't figure out how to stop The Revisionists, everything he'd worked for would be lost. And maybe, just maybe, so would the world he'd once known.

"We find the truth," Ethan said, his voice quiet but resolute. "No matter what it takes."

Felicity nodded, determination settling in her features. "Then let's get to work."

As she left the room, Ethan felt the weight of the task ahead of him pressing down on his shoulders. The missing trial was just the beginning. Whatever was happening, whatever The Revisionists were doing, it was bigger than anything he could have imagined. And the deeper he went, the more certain he became: the world was shifting beneath their feet, and the people in power were doing everything they could to control it.

But Ethan wasn't going to let them rewrite history. Not without a fight.

Thirteen

Samira's Role

The evening air was thick with the weight of unanswered questions, and Ethan Voss felt the oppressive quiet of his apartment, the silence broken only by the faint hum of his refrigerator and the distant sounds of the city outside. He leaned over his cluttered desk, the chaotic mess of papers and open files a testament to the spiraling investigation that was consuming his every waking hour. The more he uncovered, the deeper the rabbit hole went, and it felt like there was no way out.

A knock at the door broke his thoughts.

Ethan stood, muscles stiff from hours hunched over his desk, and made his way to the door. He didn't need to ask who it was. Samira Cross had been the only one willing to stick by him. The only one who believed in the case when everyone else had either backed away or vanished.

He opened the door, finding her standing in the hallway, her figure framed by the dim light from the stairwell. Her eyes, usually sharp with determination, were clouded with something darker tonight—concern, maybe, or maybe something more ominous.

"Samira," Ethan greeted, his voice rough from hours of questioning his own sanity.

"I came as soon as I could," she said, stepping inside and glancing at the mess in his apartment. "You're still at it?"

Ethan nodded but didn't speak. He moved aside, letting her pass into the room. She tossed her bag onto the couch and turned to face him, her expression a mixture of impatience and worry.

"We need to talk," Ethan said finally, his voice low. "I've been digging into something that doesn't add up. A trial—well, a trial that doesn't exist, but the evidence ties it to some powerful political figures. These names, Samira, they're all connected to high-level people in the system."

She raised an eyebrow, leaning against the desk as she crossed her arms. "A trial that never happened, but it's connected to people who have the means to make it vanish? That sounds familiar."

Ethan winced at the understatement. "There's more. I'm not the only one investigating. There's someone else—someone with the kind of power to remove entire cases from history. I don't know how they're doing it yet, but it's bigger than just a few missing records."

Samira's eyes narrowed. "Are we talking about the same people who erased Caldwell's trial?"

"Yes," he replied, the word feeling like a lead weight in his chest. "The same people. But they're doing more than just erasing individual cases. They're rewriting everything.

Memories, identities... even entire histories. And it's not just isolated incidents. This goes back years, maybe decades."

Samira didn't speak immediately. Instead, she walked over to the desk, picked up one of the files, and started flipping through it with deliberate movements. Ethan knew she was trying to connect the dots in her own way, as she always did. He let her, knowing she would come to the same conclusions he had.

"What are you suggesting?" she finally asked, stopping at a page and staring at it intently.

"I'm suggesting that someone is deliberately manipulating the legal system to erase the truth. They're rewriting history—altering the very fabric of our reality to cover up their crimes," Ethan said, his voice thick with the weight of his words.

Samira glanced up, meeting his eyes. There was a flicker of disbelief, quickly suppressed by the stoic mask she wore so well. "And you think it's the same people who erased Caldwell's trial?"

"I know it's the same people. And I'm starting to think it's not just one case. It's a whole network, a system. The Revisionists," he added, his voice trailing off as the name rolled off his tongue like a curse.

"Right," Samira said slowly, her fingers tapping the file on the desk. "The Revisionists. We've been hearing whispers about them, but no one's ever been able to prove they exist."

"They exist," Ethan said, the certainty in his voice making it feel like a fact. "They're real, Samira. And they've been manipulating the legal system for years, if not longer. Erasing inconvenient truths, wiping people from existence. We're not just dealing with some rogue faction. We're dealing with a highly organized, highly powerful group."

Samira sighed, her hand dropping to her side. "And you

think this is what's been happening to all the cases we've been investigating? Caldwell's trial, the missing witnesses, the erased memories? It's all connected."

Ethan nodded. "I don't have all the answers yet, but I'm starting to see the pattern. Everything is connected. The people who are disappearing… the cases that are being erased… It's all tied to this network. They're not just erasing crimes—they're erasing people's lives. Rewriting everything so it suits their narrative."

Samira stared at him for a long moment, her eyes filled with uncertainty and something else—something like fear. She opened her mouth to speak, but the words seemed to catch in her throat.

Ethan could see the hesitation in her expression. He knew what she was thinking. They were both in too deep now, too entangled in something that could destroy their careers, their lives, everything they'd ever known. But the truth was staring them in the face, and it was something neither of them could ignore.

"Samira," Ethan said quietly, his voice softer now. "You don't have to do this. You don't have to get involved. I can go after them alone."

Her lips pressed together in a thin line, and for a moment, Ethan thought she might actually walk away. But then she took a deep breath, as if steeling herself for what came next, and looked him in the eye.

"No," she said firmly, her tone resolute. "You're right. We're already involved. And I'm not backing down. If these people are erasing history, changing the world around us, we have to stop them. Not just for us, but for everyone they're hurting."

Ethan felt a flicker of relief. There was something about

Samira's Role

Samira that made him believe in the cause, even when the odds seemed impossible. Her sense of justice, her unwavering commitment to the truth—it was a fire that burned in both of them. And now, they were aligned. They would face this together.

"I'll help you," Samira continued, her voice steady. "But we need to know everything. We can't just keep picking at the edges. We need to go after the heart of this thing, find out who's behind it, and expose them for what they really are."

Ethan's pulse quickened. "We can do this, Samira. We just need to keep pushing. One step at a time."

She nodded, her gaze turning sharp as she picked up a fresh stack of files and handed them to him. "You've been looking at the legal angle. I'll look into the media side. If someone's been manipulating the truth, we need to know who's been covering it up."

Ethan took the files, feeling the weight of the next phase of their investigation pressing down on him. "Voryx Technologies," he said quietly, almost as if to himself. "There's a connection there. I think they're tied into all of this somehow. The technology they're developing could be used to alter memories, records... history."

Samira's eyes flickered with recognition. "Voryx. Langston's company. The AI."

Ethan nodded. "I think they're more involved than we realize. Langston has the power and the resources to make this happen. We need to find out exactly how Voryx is tied to the Revisionists. I think they're using their technology to manipulate reality itself."

"I'll see what I can find," Samira said. "But be careful, Ethan. The deeper we go, the more dangerous this gets."

Ethan met her gaze, determination hardening in his chest. "I'm already in too deep to turn back. And now, so are you."

With that, they both knew there was no turning back. The investigation had begun, and with it came the terrifying realization that the forces they were about to face were far more powerful than anything they could have ever imagined.

Fourteen

The Witness Who Wasn't

Ethan Voss leaned back in his chair, rubbing his temples as he stared at the file in front of him. The case had taken a turn that even he, in all his years of investigative work, had never seen before. A witness had emerged—out of nowhere.

There was no history. No birth certificate. No prior employment records. No trace of existence before today. And yet, this person had come forward with information that could crack everything open.

It didn't make sense.

The message had arrived that morning, tucked into the usual pile of case files that Felicity had managed to dig up for him. There was no return address, no sender name. Just a single sheet of paper, slightly yellowed as if it had been typed years ago, with a cryptic note scrawled in thick black ink.

"The answers you seek can be found through Daniel

Reese. He was there. He saw everything."

Daniel Reese.

Ethan had read the name at least a dozen times, rolling it around in his mind, trying to place it. But it was useless—there was no record of him. No files. No case notes. Nothing in the police databases or any government records. Daniel Reese didn't exist.

And yet, an hour ago, a call had come through from a burner number.

"Ethan Voss?" a man's voice had said.

Ethan had barely managed to confirm before the voice continued, low and urgent.

"I know about the missing trial. The erased witnesses. The Revisionists. Meet me at 402 Crestwell Avenue in one hour. Come alone."

Then the line had gone dead.

Ethan hadn't hesitated. He'd grabbed his coat, his gun, and a spare recorder before heading out into the cold, winding streets of Westfall.

Now, as he stood outside the abandoned apartment complex at the address given, his gut churned with the same unease that had been growing since the moment he first got the call.

Something was wrong.

He scanned the area, his eyes sharp as he took in the surroundings. The building was a relic of forgotten times, its paint peeling, the windows either shattered or covered in grime. A single flickering streetlamp cast long shadows on the cracked pavement. The kind of place where secrets came to die.

The front door hung slightly open.

Ethan reached for his gun instinctively, the weight of it reassuring as he pushed the door open and stepped inside.

The Witness Who Wasn't

The interior was worse than the exterior—dust thick in the air, the scent of mildew clinging to every surface. His footsteps echoed as he moved cautiously through the dimly lit hallway. Somewhere in the distance, water dripped, the sound eerily rhythmic.

He checked the first door on his left. Empty.

The second.

Nothing.

And then, just as he reached the end of the hall, his pulse spiked.

The last door stood slightly ajar, light spilling out from within.

Ethan raised his gun and nudged the door open with the toe of his boot.

Inside, the room was almost completely bare—except for the body slumped against the wall.

Ethan's heart pounded as he stepped inside, his breath coming faster.

The man was young, late twenties at most, with short brown hair and an average build. His hands were limp at his sides, his head tilted at an unnatural angle. A single bullet hole marred the center of his forehead, the blood still fresh.

Ethan didn't need a coroner to confirm it—this was Daniel Reese.

Or at least, whoever Daniel Reese was supposed to be.

His mind raced. He had only received the call an hour ago. Which meant that someone—whoever had arranged this meeting—had gotten to Reese first.

Had he been real at all?

Ethan crouched beside the body, his trained eyes scanning for anything that might tell him who this man really was. He checked the pockets—empty. No wallet, no ID. No phone.

It was as if Daniel Reese had never existed.

Ethan's jaw tightened as he pulled out his phone and dialed Samira.

She picked up on the second ring.

"Tell me you're somewhere safe," she said without preamble.

Ethan exhaled sharply. "Define 'safe.'"

There was a pause. "What happened?"

"I'm at Crestwell Avenue," he said. "Daniel Reese is dead."

A sharp intake of breath. "Who the hell is Daniel Reese?"

"That's the problem," Ethan muttered, standing up. "There's no record of him. Anywhere. And now, someone made sure that if there ever was, it's gone."

"Are you saying—"

"I'm saying I don't think this man ever existed, Samira." Ethan turned, scanning the room once more. "No fingerprints. No ID. No history. Just a name on a note that led me here."

Silence stretched between them for a moment before Samira spoke again, her voice low.

"This is exactly what happened with Caldwell's case," she said. "The witnesses vanished, the records erased. Ethan, if this man was created out of thin air just to be erased, we're looking at something far worse than we thought."

Ethan knew she was right.

This wasn't just about covering up a case anymore. Someone had fabricated an entire person—just to eliminate them.

That meant someone had gone through the trouble of planting his name, creating just enough of a presence to lure Ethan into following the lead, and then wiping him from reality before he could ever say a word.

But why?

Ethan's hand tightened around his phone. "They wanted me to see this," he murmured.

"What do you mean?"

"They wanted me to find him dead. To send a message." He exhaled sharply. "I think this whole thing was staged. The note. The phone call. Everything. Someone's watching us, Samira. They know we're getting too close."

The thought sent a chill down his spine.

He took one last glance at the body before he turned and made his way back down the hallway, stepping out into the cold night air. His mind raced as he walked to his car, the city lights flickering in the distance like a mirage.

They weren't just up against a cover-up anymore.

They were up against people who could rewrite reality itself.

He slid into the driver's seat, gripping the wheel tightly.

Whoever The Revisionists were, they had power that stretched far beyond what he had imagined. They didn't just erase people.

They created them.

And that meant no one—no memory, no piece of evidence—could ever be trusted.

Not even his own.

As he started the engine, his phone buzzed with a new message.

UNKNOWN NUMBER: *You were warned, Voss. Next time, we erase you.*

Ethan stared at the screen, a slow dread creeping over him.

He wasn't just an investigator anymore.

He was the next target.

Fifteen

Disappearing Clues

E than's breath hitched as he stared at the empty space in front of him. The board was gone. The photos, the notes, the connections—everything he'd spent days meticulously piecing together had vanished without a trace.

The room felt colder than it should. The overhead lights buzzed, the hum scraping against his nerves like fingernails on a chalkboard. Ethan stood in the middle of the small, cluttered office, his hands trembling as he ran them over the blank, barren surface of the wall.

For weeks, the board had been his anchor. The links between people—victims, suspects, witnesses—his tentative understanding of the conspiracy that had already claimed so many lives, had been laid out like a map, scattered with clues that he could follow, dig into, and pursue. But now...

Gone.

The connections were erased, just like everything else.

Disappearing Clues

Ethan felt the ground shift beneath him. His heart rate quickened, his thoughts becoming a whirlwind as panic clawed at him. He reached for his phone, hands fumbling, and called the one person he could trust.

Samira.

The line rang twice before her voice came through, steady, calm.

"Ethan?" she said, her tone laced with immediate concern. "What's wrong?"

"I—" His voice cracked. "I can't... Samira, the board. Everything—it's gone."

There was a long pause on the other end. He could hear her exhale, the weight of his words sinking in. "What do you mean, gone?"

"I mean it's not there. It's like someone walked in and took everything. All the connections, the faces, the names, the notes—all of it. It's like it never existed."

Samira didn't respond at first. She was no doubt processing the absurdity of his words, trying to ground them in some form of reality.

"Are you sure?" she asked, her voice tinged with a hint of doubt that she was trying to hide.

Ethan's frustration surged. "I'm standing in the middle of the office, Samira. It's like—like nothing ever happened. I'm not crazy."

He could hear the rustling of papers on her end. She was working, trying to multitask, but she didn't say anything for a while. Then:

"I'll be there in twenty minutes. We'll figure this out."

Ethan ended the call without a word. His hand hung limply by his side, the phone still cold against his skin.

Twenty minutes later, Samira stood in the doorway, her eyes scanning the office as if she could will the missing evidence back into existence. She walked toward the blank wall where the board had been and stared at it. Ethan was already pacing, his mind swirling in frustration.

"They were here," he muttered, "I swear to God, Samira, they were here. All the names, the dates, the connections—they all made sense. And now—"

"And now," Samira interrupted, her voice calm but firm, "it's like someone hit a reset button. So, tell me what's really going on here."

"I don't know anymore," Ethan said, rubbing his face with both hands. "I've been digging into this for weeks. I thought we were getting somewhere, that we were starting to understand what the hell is going on, and then—this." He motioned wildly to the empty office.

Samira didn't flinch. She knew that Ethan had been relentless in his pursuit of the truth, and this sudden disappearance of all his hard work was more than just a setback. It was a direct attack.

"Okay, we start over," she said quietly, crossing her arms. "What have we found so far?"

Ethan dragged over a chair and collapsed into it. "We've found that people—people in positions of power—are being erased. Not just their records, but their existence. Witnesses, jurors, judges—every person connected to a case like this is being systematically replaced. As if they never were."

Samira raised an eyebrow. "You think someone's erasing history?"

"Not just history," Ethan said, his voice growing more urgent, "they're rewriting reality itself. It's like we're all living in

Disappearing Clues

someone else's version of the truth."

Samira took a step forward, her eyes sharp. "So, you're saying all of this—everything we've uncovered—has been manipulated from the start?"

"Yes," Ethan replied. "And I think it's bigger than just one case or even one person. Whoever's behind this has the ability to change everything. To make people disappear. To alter facts. And they're getting better at it."

A knock on the door interrupted the tension between them. Samira's hand instinctively went to the drawer where her gun was stashed, but Ethan shook his head. "It's probably just the building manager. We're not the only ones who've had strange things happen."

He stood and went to the door, his hand on the knob. When he opened it, however, no one was there. Just a small envelope, slipped under the crack, resting at his feet.

Ethan picked it up, a sense of foreboding creeping up his spine. He glanced back at Samira, who was already on alert.

"Another one," he muttered.

He opened the envelope. Inside was a single photograph—a crime scene image that looked eerily familiar. But something was different this time.

In the center of the photo was a man, his face obscured by shadows, his body twisted in an unnatural position, blood pooling around him. He looked familiar, but there was no way to place him.

"Who is this?" Samira asked, her voice almost a whisper.

"I don't know," Ethan replied, but he was lying. He felt a sickening recognition stirring in the pit of his stomach. "This man... I've seen him before."

Samira leaned closer, studying the photo with a growing

sense of unease. "Where?"

"I don't know." His voice cracked. "It's like... it's like I should know who he is. But I can't remember."

"Ethan," Samira said, her voice growing serious, "what if it's you?"

He froze, his stomach dropping. The image was grainy, unclear, but the silhouette seemed to match his build. His heart skipped a beat, and for the first time since this whole nightmare had begun, doubt gnawed at him.

"What if," Samira continued, her voice almost too quiet, "someone's erasing you too?"

The thought struck Ethan like a punch to the gut. He had been trying to figure out the bigger picture—who was behind this, why people were disappearing, why reality was breaking apart—but had he been too close to the truth? Was he now part of the conspiracy he had been fighting?

"I need to check something," Ethan said, his voice tight with sudden urgency. "I need to check something back at my place."

Ethan's apartment felt like a stranger's house when he walked through the door. It wasn't the familiar clutter, the half-empty coffee mugs, the old newspapers stacked by the door. No, the change was more subtle. The way his shoes no longer sat where he always left them, or the way the light flickered in the hallway like a faulty memory.

He walked into the living room, eyes scanning. And there, sitting on the coffee table, was another envelope.

This time, the note inside was different. It was a single sentence.

"You're already gone."

Ethan's breath caught in his throat. The reality of the words hit him like a punch. He had been so focused on the external forces—the Revisionists, the manipulation of history—that he hadn't considered the most horrifying possibility of all.

What if he was the one being erased? What if his own identity was being rewritten, along with the people around him?

"What if I'm already gone?"

It was Samira's voice, echoing in his mind. But the thought lingered, chilling him to the core. The lines between what was real and what wasn't were blurring faster than he could keep up with. And the more he uncovered, the less he was certain of anything.

The disappearance of the board. The photos. The messages. His own memories.

He was being erased—slowly but surely.

And soon, no one would remember who Ethan Voss was.

He was already fading.

And there was nothing he could do to stop it.

Sixteen

The Fractured Mind

Ethan Voss sat alone in his dimly lit office, his mind a tangled mess of thoughts that refused to untangle themselves. The days had blended together, a blur of questions and unanswered leads. The deeper he delved into the conspiracy, the more it felt as though he were sinking into a pit with no escape. It was as if every answer led to another question, every clue vanished before he could grasp it fully.

He stared at the blank wall where his board had once been. The map of faces, names, and connections—now gone, erased by forces he didn't understand. The weight of it all crushed him, an invisible force that made it hard to breathe. His head ached, a sharp, pulsing pain that throbbed with every passing second. It felt like his mind was slipping, the very foundation of his thoughts cracking beneath him.

A knock on the door startled him, the sharp sound cutting through the oppressive silence of the room.

"Ethan?" Samira's voice called out, tentative yet firm. She had been checking on him more often lately, sensing the strain he was under.

Ethan stood up slowly, his legs unsteady as if the floor beneath him was shifting. He hadn't slept in days, his body fueled only by the adrenaline of the investigation and the gnawing fear that he was being erased from existence. What was real anymore? The faces, the places, the events—nothing felt certain.

He reached the door and opened it to find Samira standing there, her expression concerned but masked with a professionalism she always wore in the field. She was a pillar of stability, but even her presence couldn't steady the chaos inside him.

"Are you okay?" she asked quietly, her eyes scanning his face. Ethan wanted to lie, to say everything was fine, but he couldn't bring himself to do it.

"No," he muttered, his voice hoarse. "I don't think I'm okay."

Samira stepped inside, her gaze lingering on him for a moment before moving to the empty wall, where the remnants of his investigation once stood. She didn't ask what happened to it—she didn't need to. The tension between them had shifted over the past few days. They both knew something larger was at play, something that was bigger than either of them.

"Talk to me, Ethan," Samira said, her tone soft yet insistent. She stepped closer, crossing the small space between them. "What's going on in your head?"

Ethan tried to focus on her words, but they felt distant, as though they were coming from behind a thick fog. His vision blurred, the edges of the room swirling and distorting as if reality itself was being bent and reshaped. He closed his eyes, trying to steady himself, but all he could see were flashes—fragments of scenes, faces that didn't belong, whispers that echoed in his ears.

"I'm losing it, Samira," he said, his voice barely a whisper. "I don't know what's real anymore. I keep seeing things... hearing things."

Samira's expression shifted, her concern deepening. She moved toward him, placing a hand gently on his arm. "You're under a lot of pressure. The Revisionists—they've been manipulating everything. But you're still in control. You've got to believe that."

"I don't know if I am in control," Ethan muttered. He could feel the ground beneath him trembling, the walls closing in. "What if this is all... part of their game? What if they're messing with my head, too?"

Samira didn't reply immediately. Instead, she studied him closely, her gaze sharp. "You've been running on empty for days, Ethan. Maybe you need to step back for a while. Take a break. Get some rest."

Rest. The word seemed foreign to him, like a distant dream. He hadn't slept properly in weeks, his nights filled with nightmares that felt like memories from lives he didn't remember living. He was haunted by the image of the faceless man from the photo—the man he had once believed was a witness, a key to unraveling the conspiracy. Now, he wondered if the man had ever existed at all.

Before he could respond, his phone rang, the shrill sound slicing through the tension in the room. Samira's hand remained on his arm as he fumbled to grab the phone from his desk.

The name on the screen made his stomach drop.

Jonas.

He answered quickly, his heart racing. "Jonas?"

The Fractured Mind

"Ethan," Jonas's voice was strained, urgent. "You need to get to the lab. Now. Something's gone wrong. It's about the photos."

The photos. Ethan's chest tightened. "What do you mean, something's gone wrong?"

"I can't explain it over the phone," Jonas said, his voice barely controlled. "Just get here. It's important."

Without hesitation, Ethan hung up and turned to Samira. "We need to go. Now."

She didn't argue, grabbing her coat and following him out the door. The air outside was cold, biting at his skin as they made their way to the car. Samira didn't speak as they drove, but Ethan could feel the tension between them. He was on edge, his mind racing with possibilities. What could Jonas have found? Was it a breakthrough? Or had they just stumbled into another trap set by The Revisionists?

The drive felt like it took hours, the streets around them twisting and distorting as if they were caught in a nightmare. The city lights flickered in and out of focus, and for a brief moment, Ethan swore he saw a figure standing in the shadows. His heart skipped a beat, but when he blinked, the figure was gone.

He shook his head, trying to clear the fog that clung to his thoughts.

They arrived at the lab, the familiar building standing in stark contrast to the chaos inside Ethan's mind. Jonas was waiting for them outside, his expression grim.

"What's going on?" Ethan asked, his voice sharp.

Jonas didn't answer right away, instead leading them inside. The lab was dimly lit, the fluorescent lights buzzing overhead. Ethan's eyes darted around the room, taking in the stacks of files, the computers, the array of equipment. But it all seemed distant, like he was looking at it through a foggy window.

Jonas led them to a desk in the back, where several photos were scattered. Ethan's breath caught in his throat when he saw them. They were crime scene photos—disturbing, grotesque. But there was something wrong with them, something off.

In each of the photos, the victim was someone he recognized. Or at least, he thought he did.

One photo showed a man lying on the floor, blood pooling around him, his body contorted in an unnatural way. The man's face was obscured by shadows, but Ethan swore he had seen him before. The second photo was of a woman, her body splayed out in an abandoned alley, her face eerily blank.

"I've never seen these people," Samira said, her voice distant as she leaned in to inspect the photos. "Who are they?"

Ethan couldn't speak. His heart pounded in his chest, and his vision blurred. He felt his knees begin to buckle beneath him, and before he could stop himself, he was on the floor, his hands clutching his head as pain shot through his skull.

"Ethan?" Samira's voice was a muffled sound, as if coming from far away.

The room spun, and for a moment, everything went dark.

When he opened his eyes, he was no longer in the lab. He was standing in the middle of a crime scene, the same one from the photos. The body of the man lay before him, blood staining the floor. The air smelled of copper and decay.

He looked around, and then he saw it. A figure standing in the corner of the room, watching him. The figure was tall, shrouded in shadows, their face obscured.

"Who are you?" Ethan shouted, but the figure didn't respond.

The ground beneath him trembled again, and suddenly,

everything shifted. The room distorted, and the figure faded into the darkness. Ethan's heart raced as he stumbled, unsure of where he was or what was real.

"Ethan! Get up!" Samira's voice broke through the chaos.

He blinked, and the lab was back. He was lying on the floor, his hands trembling as they gripped the cold tile. Samira was crouched beside him, her expression a mixture of concern and confusion.

"What's happening to me?" Ethan whispered, his voice hoarse.

Samira didn't answer right away. She simply helped him to his feet, her hands steady as she guided him to a chair. Ethan's mind was a storm, a whirlwind of images and sounds that didn't belong. The hallucinations were growing stronger, more frequent. Was he losing his grip on reality?

"I don't know," Samira said softly, her voice filled with uncertainty. "But we need to figure this out, Ethan. Before it's too late."

Ethan could only nod, though he wasn't sure if he was still in control. The fear gnawed at him—fear that he was being erased, that his mind was fracturing piece by piece. And there was nothing he could do to stop it.

Seventeen

The New Photo

The silence in Ethan Voss's office was deafening, broken only by the soft hum of the fluorescent lights above. The weight of his thoughts pressed heavily on his shoulders, each one sinking deeper into his mind, a reminder of how close he was to losing everything. He had thought that the madness of his investigation had reached its peak, that the twisted web of the Revisionists could not get any worse. But each day had proven him wrong. The closer he got to the truth, the more fragmented his perception of reality became.

Samira had left hours ago, telling him she'd be back in the morning. She had been trying to reassure him, telling him that he was just under too much stress, that the hallucinations, the disorienting dreams—those were all symptoms of exhaustion. But Ethan knew better. The truth was darker than that. Something bigger was happening. Something that was slowly chipping away at his sanity.

The New Photo

He stared at the empty desk in front of him, the pile of files a constant reminder of the work he had yet to finish. His mind was still haunted by the faces from the photos Jonas had shown him—the bodies of strangers who looked disturbingly familiar. He had tried to push the images from his mind, but they lingered like shadows that refused to be shaken off.

Suddenly, his phone vibrated, slicing through the heavy silence. The screen flashed with an unknown number. Ethan's heart skipped a beat. It was too late for anyone to be calling with good news.

He answered the call, his voice hoarse, barely able to mask the tension. "Ethan Voss."

"Ethan," a voice crackled through the line. It was Jonas, but there was something in his tone that immediately set Ethan on edge. "I need you to get over here. Now. Something's... wrong."

Ethan's breath caught in his throat. "What is it?"

"I can't explain over the phone. Just get here, quickly."

Without hesitation, Ethan slammed the phone down and grabbed his jacket. The sense of urgency in Jonas's voice sent a chill through him. Something had changed. He could feel it in his bones.

The drive to the lab felt like an eternity. The streets blurred past him, the city lights flashing in and out of focus, as if mocking his frantic thoughts. He gripped the steering wheel so tightly his knuckles turned white. The air outside was colder than usual, biting at his skin, a constant reminder that something was coming—something he wasn't ready for.

When he finally arrived, Jonas was waiting for him outside. His expression was grim, and his hands shook slightly as he handed Ethan an envelope.

"Here," Jonas said, his voice low. "It's here."

Ethan took the envelope, feeling an unsettling weight settle in his stomach. The envelope was thick, the paper crinkled and worn, as though it had been through a lot before landing in his hands. He tore it open, his fingers trembling. Inside was a single photograph, the edges curling slightly as if it had been passed through many hands.

At first glance, Ethan thought it was just another crime scene photo, another victim, another face in the shadows. But as his eyes adjusted to the details, his breath caught in his chest. The photo was too familiar—too personal.

There he was, lying on the cold, concrete floor, a pool of blood spreading around him like a dark halo. His face was pale, his eyes open but glazed, staring into nothingness. His body was positioned unnaturally, as if someone had placed him there, posed him for a moment of finality.

But it wasn't the sight of his own lifeless body that shook him. It was the people standing around him—people he had never seen before. They were staring at him, watching him, their faces cold and indifferent. He didn't recognize them. Not one of them.

Ethan's pulse quickened as the truth of the photo began to sink in. This wasn't just another clue. This wasn't some random victim who had been erased from history. No, this was him. This was his death. And the worst part? It was happening in the present, right in front of his eyes.

His hands shook as he held the photo, his mind racing. Who were these people? Why were they surrounding his body? And more importantly—how did someone know what he would look like when he died? Was this some sort of sick game? Or was it a warning?

He looked up at Jonas, his voice barely a whisper. "Who took

The New Photo

this?"

"I don't know," Jonas replied, his voice strained. "We found it in the files. We had no idea it was coming, but it's not the first time someone's seen something like this. It's—"

Jonas stopped himself, his eyes flicking to the envelope in Ethan's hand.

Ethan's mind was racing, unable to grasp the full weight of the situation. He had never felt more exposed, more vulnerable. The sense of inevitability that had been lurking in the background for days now took center stage. He was being hunted. And someone knew exactly how his story would end.

Jonas's voice broke through his thoughts. "We need to figure out who's behind this, Ethan. The Revisionists—they're getting closer. We can't keep playing this game. Not if they're watching you like this."

Ethan snapped his head up, his eyes burning with the intensity of his resolve. "They want me dead, Jonas. This photo—it's not just a threat. It's a blueprint."

Jonas hesitated. "But how—how do they know this much? How could they have taken a photo of something that hasn't happened yet?"

Ethan felt a shiver run down his spine. "They're rewriting history. They're not just erasing people—they're planning how we're going to be erased. They're pulling the strings, manipulating everything. They're in control of the story, Jonas. And they're making sure that I'm part of it."

Jonas swallowed hard, his face pale. "So, what now?"

Ethan clenched his fists, the photo still gripped tightly in his hand. His mind was working in overdrive, the pieces of the puzzle falling into place, but the picture it was forming was far darker than anything he had anticipated.

"I need to get to Samira," Ethan said, his voice hard with determination. "She needs to see this."

The drive to Samira's place was brief, but every second felt like an eternity. His mind churned, trying to process everything, to piece together a plan. The photo was a message, an ominous one. Whoever had sent it knew what would happen to him—and they wanted him to know that too.

When he arrived at Samira's apartment, he didn't waste any time. He knocked once, then pushed open the door. Samira was sitting at the kitchen table, her back to him, scribbling notes on a notepad. She turned as he entered, her expression neutral until she saw the look on his face.

"What's wrong?" she asked, sensing the change in him immediately.

Ethan held up the photograph, wordlessly handing it to her. Samira took it, her brow furrowing as she studied it. Her eyes flickered between Ethan and the photo, her expression growing more troubled with each passing second.

"Where did you get this?" Samira asked, her voice low.

"I don't know," Ethan replied, pacing the small room. "Jonas found it. But that's not the point, Samira. Look at the photo. Look at the people around me."

Samira glanced at the photo again, her face unreadable. She set it down on the table, meeting Ethan's gaze. "These people... they're not from any of your cases. I've never seen them before."

Ethan nodded. "Neither have I. But it's not just that. It's me, Samira. I'm the one lying on the floor. The photo's of me. Dead."

Samira's eyes widened. "Dead?"

"Yes. And whoever's behind this... they're planning it. They know how and when it's going to happen. And they're making

The New Photo

sure I see it. That's the part I don't understand. They want me to know."

The room was heavy with the weight of their silence. Samira took a deep breath, her eyes narrowing. "Ethan, we're running out of time. We need to find out who's doing this. And why."

Ethan felt the chill of dread settle in his bones. The photo was no longer just a symbol of danger—it was a sign. A sign that he was next, that the clock was ticking, and that everything he had worked for might be nothing more than a carefully constructed illusion.

"I'll find them, Samira," Ethan said, his voice filled with cold resolve. "I'll find the people who are doing this, even if it's the last thing I do."

As he turned to leave, the photo still burned in his mind, the image of his own body lying lifeless on the floor. The truth was closing in around him, and with it, the terrifying realization that he was not just chasing a conspiracy. He was its next victim.

Eighteen

Felicity's Dilemma

The weight of the world seemed to press down on Felicity Harris as she sat in her office, the familiar hum of the city filtering through the window like a distant echo. The sun was just beginning to dip beneath the horizon, casting a warm glow across the room, but the light felt like a cruel illusion. The room, filled with stacks of legal files, felt more like a prison than a place of refuge. The walls, once comforting with their familiarity, now seemed to close in on her, trapping her in the very system she had spent years devoted to.

Her fingers hovered over the keyboard of her laptop, but she couldn't bring herself to type. The documents on the screen were not just another pile of cases to be reviewed—they were the proof of something that she had long suspected but had never fully dared to believe. The Revisionists, the secret society that had been manipulating the very fabric of justice, had left their fingerprints all over these cases. The records, the witnesses, the verdicts—they had all been twisted, altered, erased.

She leaned back in her chair, staring at the ceiling, as the weight of the decision she had to make pressed down on her. How could she continue to practice law knowing that the system was rigged? That the very laws she had sworn to uphold were being used as tools for manipulation, to bend reality to fit the will of a hidden, powerful few? How could she ignore the undeniable truth that had come crashing into her life like a freight train, and more importantly, how could she continue to live with herself if she did nothing about it?

Felicity had always believed in the law. It was her faith, her foundation. She had worked tirelessly to climb the ladder of success in one of the most prestigious law firms in the city, always convinced that justice was not just a concept but a tangible force. But now, as the evidence piled up, she realized that justice wasn't a force at all—it was a commodity, a tool wielded by those who held the most power.

Her phone buzzed, interrupting the storm of thoughts in her mind. She picked it up without thinking, already knowing who it was before she even glanced at the screen. Ethan. The man who had been at the center of her life for the past few weeks. The one who had pulled her into the darkest corners of the truth. The one who had shown her that the world she had believed in was nothing but a house of cards, ready to collapse under its own weight.

She pressed the green button to answer the call. "Ethan?"

"Felicity," his voice came through, tight with urgency. "I need to see you. It's about the case. You won't believe what we've uncovered."

His words hung in the air, and Felicity felt her pulse quicken. She knew he wasn't exaggerating. This was the moment she had been dreading. The moment when the truth was no longer something she could ignore or push aside. It had been creeping up on her for weeks, but now it was here, forcing her to confront the impossible choice she had to make.

"I'm on my way," she said, her voice steady despite the whirlwind inside her. She couldn't run from this. Not anymore.

The drive to the small office Ethan had been using for their investigation felt longer than it should have, the streets blurring in her mind as her thoughts circled back to the dilemma she faced. Could she truly abandon the legal system she had worked so hard to be a part of? Could she turn her back on the very thing that had defined her for so long? She had always believed that she was fighting for justice, but now it seemed like the battle was rigged from the start. The very people she had once considered allies were the ones who had been pulling the strings, manipulating the game from behind the scenes.

But then there was Ethan. Ethan, who had risked everything to uncover the truth. Ethan, who had been dragged into the darkness but still fought to expose the lies. He had been a light in a world of shadows, a constant reminder of the possibility of redemption, even in a system so corrupted by power.

She parked her car and walked briskly to the building where Ethan was waiting. Her heart pounded in her chest, and with every step, the weight of her decision grew heavier. She was about to walk into a world where there were no easy answers, no clear right or wrong. And yet, deep down, she knew what she had to do. She couldn't ignore the truth any longer. She couldn't stay silent and let the powerful continue to manipulate the law, erasing and rewriting history with no consequences.

Felicity's Dilemma

As she entered the building, she found Ethan standing near a desk, looking through a stack of files. His expression was tense, his eyes shadowed with the weight of the investigation. He looked up as she entered, and for a moment, the two of them simply stared at each other, the silence between them thick with unspoken understanding.

"You look like you've seen a ghost," Felicity said, her voice gentle, but laced with concern.

Ethan gave a tight smile, but it didn't reach his eyes. "Maybe I have," he replied, handing her a folder. "Take a look at this."

Felicity opened the folder, her breath catching as she scanned the documents inside. It was a series of case files—murder investigations, missing persons reports, and political scandals. Each one had been tampered with in some way. Some had been erased from the records completely, while others had been altered, witnesses rewritten, details shifted. The Revisionists had left their mark on each and every case, manipulating the outcomes to fit their agenda.

But what struck her the most were the names of the judges, the lawyers, the people in power who had been complicit in these alterations. People she knew. People she had worked with. People she had trusted.

Her hand trembled as she turned the pages, the truth sinking in deeper with each passing moment. She felt the walls of the legal system she had devoted herself to begin to crumble around her. What was she supposed to do now? How could she continue to practice law knowing that the very foundation she had built her career on was nothing but a facade?

"This is it, Felicity," Ethan's voice broke through her thoughts. "This is the proof we've been looking for. The Revisionists are everywhere, and they've been controlling everything. The law, the courts, the very system that's supposed to protect people—it's all been manipulated."

Felicity closed the folder, her mind racing. "I don't know what to say, Ethan. This changes everything. The system... the system I've spent my whole life defending. It's all part of the lie."

"I know," Ethan said quietly, his gaze intense. "But we can't just sit back and let them control it all. We have to expose the truth. We have to take a stand."

Her eyes met his, and in that moment, something shifted. The choice that had been gnawing at her for so long was no longer abstract. It was right in front of her, forcing her to confront the consequences of every decision she had made.

"I've spent my entire career fighting for justice," Felicity said, her voice raw. "But now I'm not sure I even know what justice is anymore."

"Justice isn't a system, Felicity," Ethan replied, his voice steady, "it's a cause. And right now, that cause is the truth. We need you. The people who have been manipulating the system—they can't be allowed to win. If we don't act now, everything will be lost."

Felicity closed her eyes, letting the weight of his words sink in. She had been living in a world where right and wrong had seemed clear-cut, but now she understood that the lines were far more blurred. The Revisionists had created a world where the truth was malleable, where everything could be rewritten to suit their needs. And she had to decide whether she would continue to be part of that system or whether she would join the fight to expose it for what it was.

"I've spent my life believing in the law," she said softly, her voice trembling with the weight of the decision. "But I can't ignore what I know now. I can't pretend that everything is fine when the system is broken beyond repair."

Ethan's eyes softened as he stepped closer, placing a hand on her shoulder. "You don't have to do this alone. We can fight this together."

Felicity took a deep breath, her heart pounding in her chest. The truth had been set before her, undeniable and harsh. She could no longer turn away from it. She could no longer hide behind the veil of a corrupt system that claimed to deliver justice when it had long since abandoned the truth.

"I'm with you," she said, her voice resolute. "Let's expose them. Let's take them down."

In that moment, Felicity made her choice. She would no longer stand by as the law was manipulated and twisted. She would fight for the truth, no matter the cost. It was a fight that would test everything she had ever believed in, but she knew one thing for sure: the only way to restore justice was to tear down the system that had failed so many—and to rebuild it from the ashes.

The fight had only just begun.

Nineteen

A Race Against Time

Ethan Voss could feel the clock ticking, each second slipping away faster than the one before. The photo—the one that showed him lying lifeless on the cold ground, surrounded by faces he didn't recognize—had haunted him for days, a constant reminder that his time was running out. But it was more than just the chilling image of his death. It was the realization that everything he had uncovered, everything he had worked for, was about to be erased. And with it, he and everyone who knew the truth would be wiped from history.

Samira and Felicity sat across from him, the three of them crowded around a table, papers and photographs strewn across its surface like a shattered puzzle. The images of the faces from the photo, the documents detailing the manipulations of The Revisionists, and the handful of leads they had tracked down all pointed to one thing: they needed to move fast. If they didn't, they too would vanish, just like the countless people before them.

"We don't have much time," Samira said, her voice steady but laced with urgency. "They're getting closer. The Revisionists have been watching us, and they know what we're after."

Ethan nodded, rubbing his eyes, trying to shake off the exhaustion that had begun to cloud his thoughts. He hadn't slept in days, the constant pressure of the investigation weighing heavily on him. But now, with everything on the line, sleep seemed like a luxury he could no longer afford.

Felicity leaned forward, her brow furrowed as she flipped through a folder filled with case files and notes they had gathered over the past few weeks. "The question is, where do we go from here? We've followed every lead, uncovered their lies, but they're still steps ahead. We need to find the key player—the person who's pulling all the strings. We need to get to the source of the photos and the technology behind the erasure of memories."

Ethan met her gaze, his eyes sharp. "We're not just looking for one person. We're looking for the technology they're using to rewrite history. The photos, the erased memories, the way they've managed to fabricate and eliminate people—it's all connected. If we can find the source, we might be able to stop them."

Samira's expression was tight with frustration. "But where? The network is vast, and they've covered their tracks well. Whoever's behind this is good—really good."

"We need to take risks," Ethan said, standing up and pacing the small room. "If we keep playing it safe, we'll be too late. We've got to hit them where it hurts."

Felicity looked up from the folder. "What do you mean?"

Ethan stopped in his tracks, turning to face her. "I think I know who the key player is. It's someone in the government, someone high up. They've been using the legal system to erase people, manipulate records, and control the narrative. They're the ones funding The Revisionists. But the question is: how do we get to them?"

Samira's eyes narrowed, her mind clearly working at full speed. "You're talking about someone in a position of power—someone who has access to the tech and the resources to make all of this possible. But we don't even know who they are. How do we track them down?"

Ethan shook his head. "We don't have all the answers, but I've got a lead. A contact who might know something about the technology they're using. If we can find this person, they'll point us in the right direction."

Felicity hesitated, her eyes filled with doubt. "And if they don't? What then?"

"We don't have a choice," Ethan said, his voice hardening with resolve. "If we don't find the source of this, we'll be erased. All of us. They've already wiped out too many people, and they won't stop until we're gone too."

Samira's gaze flickered to the door, her hand resting on the handle. "We need to go now. We're already running out of time. If we wait too long, we'll never get the chance to expose them."

Without another word, the three of them gathered their things and headed for the door, the weight of the world pressing down on their shoulders. The streets outside were dark, the city lights casting long shadows as they made their way to the car. The air was thick with the tension of what was to come. The further they went, the more Ethan could feel the eyes on them, the sense of being watched growing stronger with each step. The Revisionists were out there, lurking in the shadows, waiting for their next move.

The car ride was silent, each of them lost in their thoughts as they sped through the city streets. Ethan's mind was racing, every piece of the puzzle falling into place, but it was still incomplete. They needed the last piece—the key that would unlock everything. If they didn't find it soon, they would all be lost.

When they arrived at the address Ethan had been given, they parked the car a few blocks away, careful not to draw attention. The building in front of them was unassuming—an old, run-down warehouse on the edge of town. There was nothing special about it, except for the fact that it was the only lead they had. Ethan's contact was supposed to be inside, but he couldn't shake the feeling that it was a trap. The Revisionists had been too careful, too efficient in covering their tracks for this to be a coincidence.

"This is it," Ethan said, his voice low. "Stay close. Don't trust anyone."

They moved quickly, slipping through the alley and around the back of the warehouse, where they found a small, hidden door. Ethan knocked three times, the signal he had been given. After a few moments, the door creaked open, revealing a man standing in the doorway.

"You Ethan Voss?" the man asked, his voice raspy.

Ethan nodded. "We need to talk."

The man stepped aside, allowing them to enter. Inside, the warehouse was dark, filled with the smell of dust and decay. The only light came from a few dim bulbs hanging from the ceiling. The man led them down a narrow hallway, his footsteps echoing in the silence.

"Follow me," he said, leading them to a small room in the back.

The walls were lined with old computers, servers, and pieces of equipment Ethan couldn't recognize. It was clear that this was more than just a storage facility—it was a hub for something much bigger.

"What is this place?" Samira asked, her eyes scanning the room.

The man didn't answer immediately. He turned to face them, his expression guarded. "This is where the magic happens," he said. "You're looking for the technology behind the erasure, right?"

Ethan nodded. "You know about it?"

The man hesitated, then pulled a file from a drawer and tossed it onto the table. "I know more than you think. The Revisionists have been using this tech for years, and they've been perfecting it. But it's not just about erasing memories. It's about rewriting history itself. Changing the past, erasing people from existence, and making sure no one can ever uncover the truth."

Felicity stepped forward, her eyes wide. "How do you know all this?"

The man's face darkened. "Because I used to work for them."

Ethan's stomach tightened. "What happened? Why are you helping us?"

"I didn't have a choice," the man said, his voice low. "I got too close. I saw things I shouldn't have, and they came for me. Now I'm on the run, just like you. If you want to stop them, you need to use this." He gestured to the file on the table. "This is the key to everything. It will show you how to destroy the technology, how to break their hold over the system."

Ethan picked up the file, his fingers trembling as he flipped it open. Inside were diagrams, blueprints, and detailed notes about the technology. The Revisionists had created a system that could alter memories, erase people from history, and control every piece of information.

"This is it," Ethan said, his voice hoarse. "We can take them down."

But as he looked up, he saw something that made his blood run cold. The door to the room was slowly creaking open, and through the crack, Ethan could see shadows moving in the hallway. They weren't alone.

"They know we're here," Samira said, her voice urgent.

Ethan grabbed the file and shoved it into his bag. "We need to move, now."

They bolted for the door, but as they reached the hallway, they were met by a group of men in black suits, their faces obscured by dark glasses. The Revisionists had found them.

"This is it," Ethan said, his voice grim. "They're not going to let us leave."

But as the men advanced, Ethan knew one thing for sure—he wasn't going down without a fight. The truth had been uncovered, and no one, not even the Revisionists, could erase that.

It was a race against time, and Ethan, Samira, and Felicity had no intention of losing.

Twenty

The Final Image

Ethan Voss's heart pounded in his chest as he crouched behind the corner of the abandoned building, his breath shallow, every nerve on edge. He could feel the air pressing down on him, thick with the weight of everything that was about to happen. This was it—the final confrontation. The moment when everything would either fall into place or shatter beyond repair. His mind raced, constantly shifting between the realization of how close they were to the truth and the looming dread of what might happen if they were too late.

Samira and Felicity were with him, crouched low beside him, their faces grim with determination. They had tracked down the last piece of the puzzle, the key player behind the vast conspiracy that had been orchestrating the erasure of people, the manipulation of memories, and the rewriting of history itself. The Revisionists. The organization that had haunted every step of their investigation, lurking in the shadows, pulling strings from places far above their reach.

But now, after weeks of running, hiding, and piecing together the broken shards of truth, they had come face to face with the heart of it all. This wasn't just a fight to expose the lies—it was a fight for their very existence. If they failed now, they would be erased. And no one would remember them. Not even the truth would survive.

"Are you ready?" Samira's voice broke through the tension, her words steady but laced with urgency. She had been the one to pull them through the worst of it, the one who never flinched when the stakes seemed too high. But even now, as they closed in on their final target, Ethan could see the flicker of fear in her eyes.

"I have no choice," Ethan muttered, his voice hoarse. "We don't have time to waste. If we don't stop them now, they'll rewrite everything. They'll make sure we never existed."

Felicity nodded, her jaw tight with resolve. "We're not just doing this for us. We're doing this for everyone who's been erased, for everyone who's been forgotten. We need to expose them before it's too late."

Ethan felt a surge of gratitude for Felicity's unwavering belief in the cause, in the truth. She had come a long way from the legal professional who once trusted the system. Now, she was just as committed as he was to seeing the Revisionists' reign of terror come to an end.

They moved swiftly through the abandoned building, their footsteps quiet on the dusty floor. The building was in complete disarray, the walls covered in peeling paint, the windows shattered. It was the perfect hiding place for an organization like The Revisionists, hidden in plain sight.

Ahead, in the dim light filtering through cracks in the walls, they saw a door slightly ajar. Ethan's pulse quickened. This was it. The final room. The final confrontation.

He signaled for them to stop, and they waited for a moment, listening for any signs of movement from within. The air was thick with tension, every second stretching longer than it should have. Ethan felt his thoughts growing sharper, the adrenaline kicking in, sharpening his focus. They had come too far to turn back now.

With a steady hand, Ethan pushed the door open just enough to peek inside. What he saw took his breath away.

At the far end of the room, seated in front of a bank of computers, was a man. He looked ordinary, dressed in a dark suit, his back to them as he typed furiously on the keyboard. The low hum of machinery filled the room, the only sound breaking the oppressive silence. But Ethan knew this was no ordinary man. This was the mastermind behind the manipulation of memories, the erasure of identities, the puppet master who had been orchestrating everything from the shadows.

The man's name was Charles Ashford. A name Ethan had come across only recently, in the final pieces of the puzzle. He was a high-ranking government official, one who had been using his power to ensure the Revisionists' control over the system. The photos, the erased records, the disappearing people—it had all been Ashford's doing.

Ethan motioned for Samira and Felicity to stay back as he stepped into the room, his gun in hand, his movements silent but deliberate. He wasn't here to negotiate. He wasn't here to ask questions. They had reached the end, and it was time to confront Ashford for everything he had done.

Ashford didn't turn around when he heard the door creak open. He kept typing, his fingers moving methodically across the keys. It was almost as if he knew they were there, as if he had been waiting for them.

"I've been expecting you," Ashford said, his voice calm, almost bored.

Ethan's grip tightened on his gun, but he didn't raise it. Not yet. He needed answers first. "You've been expecting us?" Ethan's voice was low, controlled. "For how long?"

Ashford finally turned around in his chair, a smirk playing at the corners of his lips. His eyes were cold, calculating, a man who had long since stopped seeing people as anything more than tools. "Oh, I've known about you three from the beginning. I've been watching. And I've been waiting for you to figure it all out. But now that you have, it's time for the final phase."

"What final phase?" Samira asked, her voice steady but filled with barely-contained anger. "What are you planning?"

Ashford stood slowly, walking toward them with a measured, confident stride. "I'm not planning anything," he said. "I'm simply executing a plan that's been in the works for years. You three were never supposed to get this far. But you've made it interesting. And now, I'm going to make sure that none of you are ever remembered again."

The words hit Ethan like a punch to the gut. He had suspected this was coming, but hearing it out loud made the weight of it all settle in. The Revisionists weren't just erasing people—they were erasing their entire existence. Every action, every memory, every trace of them would be wiped from history.

"You can't do that," Felicity said, her voice trembling with a mix of fury and disbelief. "We won't let you."

Ashford smiled, his lips curling into a thin, cruel line. "You don't have a choice. You never did."

Ethan stepped forward, his eyes narrowing. "What's the point of all this? Why manipulate history? Why erase people like they were never here?"

Ashford's gaze flickered to the monitors behind him. "It's simple. Control. If you control history, you control the future. If you erase inconvenient people, inconvenient truths, you reshape the world as you see fit. It's the ultimate power."

The realization hit Ethan like a lightning bolt. This wasn't just about covering up mistakes or protecting secrets. This was about creating a new world, one where the Revisionists had ultimate power, where they could rewrite the narrative to serve their own needs. It was a terrifying thought, one that made everything they had uncovered seem small in comparison. The stakes had always been high, but now they were even higher.

Ashford walked over to one of the computers and pressed a few keys. The screens flickered to life, and Ethan's heart skipped a beat as he saw what was on them. It was a feed, live and grainy, showing people—some of them familiar faces, others strangers—all standing in a sterile, clinical room. They were being erased, their identities erased, their memories wiped clean as if they had never existed.

"This is how it works," Ashford said, his voice filled with a chilling sense of satisfaction. "One click, and all these people are gone. All their lives, their memories, their histories—nothing. Gone. Just like that."

Ethan felt a cold rage settle in his chest. This was it. The source of the photos, the technology behind the erasure—it was right here. But there was something more—something that made his blood run cold. Ashford wasn't just erasing people. He was erasing the very concept of them.

"You think you can control everything," Ethan said, his voice

The Final Image

tight with anger. "But you're wrong. You won't win."

Ashford turned to face him, his expression unreadable. "You still don't understand, do you, Ethan?" He gestured to the monitors, his fingers brushing the keys with a casual ease. "You and your little team have been a part of this plan all along. The photo you found, the one of you dead—it wasn't a warning. It was a message."

Ethan's pulse quickened. "What do you mean?"

Ashford smirked, his eyes gleaming with dark amusement. "I know how this ends. I know what you're going to do. And I know how you're going to fail. You see, Ethan, I've already erased you."

The words hit Ethan like a physical blow. He blinked, his vision swimming, his mind struggling to process what Ashford was saying. "What do you mean? You can't—"

Ashford raised a hand, silencing him. "You've already been erased, Ethan. Your existence is already gone. The photo wasn't a prediction—it was the truth. Your memories, your very life, will be rewritten. The world will forget about you. Just like that."

Ethan staggered back, the room spinning. He reached for his head, feeling the crushing weight of Ashford's words. Had it already happened? Was he already gone? His heart pounded in his chest, panic rising as he realized what Ashford had done.

"No," Samira whispered, her voice low. "This can't be real."

Ashford smiled darkly, his fingers hovering over the keyboard once more. "It's already happening. You're already a ghost. Your time is up, Ethan."

But just as the room seemed to close in around him, just as everything he had fought for seemed to slip through his fingers, Ethan made a decision. He wouldn't go down quietly.

He wouldn't let Ashford—or the Revisionists—rewrite his existence.

With a burst of adrenaline, Ethan lunged forward, grabbing the nearest object—a heavy metal rod—and swung it at the computer console. Sparks flew as the monitors flickered violently, the sound of crashing metal ringing in his ears.

Samira and Felicity sprang into action, grabbing whatever they could to help. There was no more time for hesitation. They weren't just fighting for their lives. They were fighting for the truth—and they weren't going to let it be erased.

Epilogue

Jonas Hale stared at the pile of case files spread across his desk, the weight of them pressing down on him with an almost physical force. The papers were crisp and cold, but the world they represented had become anything but. He had seen countless cases in his years as a lawyer—criminal defense, corporate misconduct, even a few high-profile trials—but none had ever felt quite like this. None had ever made him feel as if the ground beneath his feet was slowly crumbling away, piece by piece.

The case he had picked up a week ago, buried in the stack of files he had yet to review, had started out like any other. A promising young lawyer—confident, capable—had taken on the defense of her client, Damien Thorpe, a man who had been accused of a horrific crime he swore he did not commit. The trial had been a spectacle; the courtroom packed, the media watching closely, and the pressure of the case mounting with every passing day. It had looked like a straightforward case of justice waiting to be served. But when Jonas began to dig deeper, that's when things started to unravel.

Damien Thorpe was supposed to have been proven innocent.

The evidence, as it had been laid out in the initial stages of the trial, suggested that he had been wrongly accused. A mix-up, a conspiracy—something had gone terribly wrong, and the real culprit had slipped through the cracks. It had been a case of corruption in the system, and as Jonas dug further, he had been certain of one thing: Thorpe was innocent.

But then the files started disappearing. At first, it had been small things. Court documents, witness testimonies—files that seemed misplaced or somehow lost in the shuffle of a busy office. He didn't think much of it. But as the days went on, the situation grew increasingly strange.

The evidence of Thorpe's innocence—gone. Not just misplaced, but completely erased from existence. Surveillance footage showing his whereabouts on the night of the crime—vanished. Court documents—erased from the record. The witness statements—gone as though they had never been taken. And the most unnerving part? No one seemed to remember the trial at all. The judge, the jurors, the attorneys—none of them could recall the case, the details, or even the defendant's name. It was as if the trial had never happened.

Jonas had spent hours trying to piece together the fragmented pieces of the case, but every lead, every clue he had once thought to be solid, was slipping through his fingers like smoke. What was once a case he was sure he could win had become a dark labyrinth of erased truths, and he was trapped in the middle of it.

As Jonas flipped through the last few documents on his desk, he found himself staring at a new file, one he hadn't noticed before. It was a simple manila folder, the kind he had seen hundreds of times, but there was something off about it. He opened it slowly, his hands trembling as he scanned the first

Epilogue

page.

The name on the cover was Damien Thorpe's. But this wasn't the file he had been working on. This was a different version of the case—one where Thorpe was the guilty party. The charges against him were different, the timeline altered, the witness statements fabricated to fit a narrative that didn't align with the truth.

This was no ordinary case file. This was a rewritten version of history. A version that had been altered to serve a purpose, to bury the truth, and make Thorpe the villain in a story that wasn't even his own.

Jonas's heart sank as he flipped through the rest of the pages, each one more disturbing than the last. The evidence wasn't just missing—it had been replaced, fabricated, and manipulated to make it appear as though Thorpe had committed the crime. But none of it made sense. The deeper he dug, the more he realized that someone—or something—had been actively erasing the truth. The very foundation of the case, the foundation of reality, was being rewritten, and the more he uncovered, the closer he came to understanding that the power behind this was not just in control of the legal system—it was in control of everything.

The photo from the case he had been working on earlier flashed in his mind. The faces of the witnesses, their identities erased, their memories wiped clean. It wasn't just the legal system that had been altered. It was the very fabric of reality itself that was being manipulated, twisted, erased.

Jonas slammed the file shut, his hands shaking. He had known there was something wrong with the case from the start, but now he understood the true scope of what was happening. The Revisionists, a secret group he had only recently learned about, were not just altering legal records. They were erasing people from existence, rewriting their very memories, and controlling the future by manipulating the past.

Jonas leaned back in his chair, his mind racing. This was bigger than anything he had ever encountered before. The Revisionists were a shadowy force, operating from the dark corners of power, pulling the strings behind the scenes. And now, Jonas was caught in their web, trying desperately to untangle the truth before it swallowed him whole.

He had to find a way to stop them. To expose them for what they were and restore the reality they had so carefully crafted to their own ends. But the closer he got, the more dangerous it became. Every step forward felt like he was taking two steps back. The deeper he dug, the more pieces of his own reality began to slip away. Memories of his past, his colleagues, his family—they all began to feel distant, like they were part of a story someone else had written.

Jonas's phone buzzed, snapping him out of his thoughts. He picked it up without looking, his mind too preoccupied with the case, with the disappearing evidence, to care about anything else.

"Jonas," the voice on the other end was familiar, but distant. "You need to stop."

The words hit him like a slap in the face. "What do you mean?" he asked, his voice trembling. "I have to keep going. I have to find the truth."

"You don't understand," the voice replied, the urgency clear now. "The truth is dangerous. You're digging too deep. The Revisionists—they'll come for you next."

Jonas's heart skipped a beat. "Who is this?"

The voice didn't answer. Instead, the line went dead, leaving Jonas in a cold silence. He stared at the phone in his hand, the

Epilogue

weight of the warning settling over him like a heavy fog.

The deeper he went, the closer he came to unraveling a conspiracy that could destroy everything he believed in. The Revisionists had already begun erasing him from existence. He was already being forgotten.

And the scariest part? He didn't know if he could stop them before they erased him completely.

www.ingramcontent.com/pod-product-compliance
Lightning Source LLC
LaVergne TN
LVHW011951070526
838202LV00054B/4900